GW00976357

This book is dedicated to
my late father Stan Smollan
(10 January 1920 – 2 November 2016)

He will sadly never feel, touch or read the
published edition of this book.

G-d bless you Dad.
You will be warmly remembered by many.

You were the best friend I have ever had. I miss
your wise counsel and your wonderful sense of
humour. I miss our almost daily phone
conversations, the last of which was the day
before you passed on.
RIP

INTRODUCTION

A decade after first being declared governor of what is now northern Italy and south eastern Europe, Julius Caesar announced his intentions to the Roman Senate, with a simple act on January 10, 49 BCE. Leading a legion across the Rubicon River a few miles south of Ravenna, the popular general would create a shift in the future of Western Civilization by marching on the capital.

Exactly 1970 years later, on January 10th 1920, the same day that Stan Smollan was born in Johannesburg, South Africa, the price of silver reached an all-time record 1.37 US Dollars an ounce. This was directly influenced by the fact that on that very day, in Paris France, the Covenant of the League of Nations, ratified by 42 nations in 1919, took effect, and the League of Nations was inaugurated. This symbolically ended World War One. The intention was that all future disputes between nations should only be settled by debate and negotiation. That was 19 years before the young Stan Smollan signed up with the Transvaal Scottish Regiment of the Union Defence Force (South Africa).

LEAGUE OF NATIONS

SOCIETE DES NATIONS

Stan's resolve was to play his part in a war that was to be *a fight for lasting worldwide peace!*

BACKGROUND

Stan's father, Moss Smollan was born in Stockton, Yorkshire, England in April 1875. Stan's paternal grandparents were Polish immigrants to England.

Moss emigrated from Middlesbrough to Johannesburg South Africa. He established the Germiston College, which was one of the two first business colleges in South Africa to teach Pitmans Shorthand. Moss's cousin Morris

Smollan, had also come to South Africa, and he established The Johannesburg Business College, also teaching Pitman's Shorthand.

Moss's sister Rikah was married to Dick Harmel, who was a keyman in the Schlesinger Group.

Founder, I.W. Schlesinger came to South Africa from New York in 1894. He was fired up with ambition and became a highly successful industrialist, entrepreneur and impresario He established a massive business empire, including African Life Assurance Company Limited, which in its first year, 1904, established a world record for the sale of insurance policies.

Stan's father, Moss

In the 1940's Moss decided to form his own company Moss Smollan and Sons (Pty) Limited, as a broker. At the time he became a senior representative of African Life Assurance Limited. He also became a chief broker of Yorkshire Insurance Company Limited, England. This positioned Moss Smollan and Sons (Pty) Limited to become a major player in short term insurance, life insurance and investment in South Africa. The company continued after Moss passed away, with Stan's two older brothers, Julien and Dennis in control.

Stan's late mother, Cissie Smollan, was the daughter of Louis Isaacson, who was born in 1868 in Windau, Kurland, Latvia (then part of Russia). He emigrated to Dublin in Ireland. There he married Sarah Light in 1889.
Their wedding took place in 5 Walworth Road, Portobello, Dublin.
They lived next door at 3 Walworth Road, where they raised their children. Louis Isaacson was a deeply religious man. He held religous services at home at that address, which later became a synagogue. The Jewish Museum is today located in premises at numbers 3 and 5 Walworth Road.

The Jewish Museum at Walworth Road, Portobello, Dublin. Louis and Sarah Isaacson had four daughters; Cissie, Dinah, Hannah and Molly. They also had two sons Bernie and Solly, both of whom died in the flu epidemic of the 1890's,. The Isaacson family immigrated to Kimberley in South Africa in 1896. There Stan Smollan's grandfather, Louis Isaacson, started a wholesale business known as "L Isaacson & Sons" in Bean Street, Kimberley.

Louis Isaacson became a pillar of society. He was president of both the Synagogue in Kimberley, and of the Griqualand West Benevolent Society. He gave to all charities Jewish and non-Jewish. The Louis Isaacson Lodge of the Hebrew Order David was consecrated in 1981 in Kimberley, in his honour

Stan recalled "I fondly remember the family visiting my grandparents, in Kimberley, when I was a child. My grandfather had an artificial leg."

Julien, Stanley and Dennis Smollan

Escape To Anzio

Stan and his two brothers, Julien and Dennis, all attended Rosebank Primary School, and then Parktown Boys High School, in Johannesburg. Stan was the youngest brother.

Parktown Boys High School was founded in 1920, the year my father, Stan Smollan, was born. I was later to also attend Parktown Boys High School. In 1966, Stan and I were the first ever father and son team to attend an Old Parktonian Association Annual Dinner together.

Parktown Boys High is one of the few schools in South Africa that to this day continues with the tradition of cadets, which has always been viewed as an exemplary way of instilling discipline and team spirit into young boys. The Parktown Boys High School Cadets has been historically affiliated to the Transvaal Scottish Regiment. Over the years, The Transvaal Scottish has sent representatives to judge the annual cadet competitions at the school.

"The View"
Transvaal Scottish Regimental Head Quarters

The
Jock
Column

CHRONICLE OF THE TRANSVAAL SCOTTISH REGIMENTAL
ASSOCIATION

The Transvaal Scottish Regiment of the South African Defence Force, was later to have a strong influence on Stan Smollan and his school mates, who on South Africa's entry into World War II in September 1939, felt a resolute obligation to join the army and contribute to the war effort.

In April 2002 Stan Smollan, formerly Private Stanley Smollan, Number 27498, of the second battalion of the Transvaal Scottish Regiment of South Africa, finally parted with portion of his unique collection of documents and photographs from the Second World War. He handed over the collection to the Transvaal Scottish Regimental Association, for preservation in its then newly established museum.

Stan, then 82, was amongst the last surviving members of a daring band of Springboks who managed to escape from an Italian Prisoner of War camp, evade recapture, and finally slip through enemy lines to rejoin their Allied comrades."

Stan Smollan's True WW2 Saga **Escape To Anzio**

Parktown Boys High School & Transvaal Scottish Logos

Display cabinet in The Transvaal Scottish Museum with
part of Stan Smollan's collection from WWII

Stan Smollan at the Transvaal Scottish Museum showing
his tunic. 19th June 2015

Ruth Smollan (1920-1995)

My parents had been married for 48 years when my mother passed away.

While I was growing up, and indeed until I was in my late forties, Dad reticently spoke very little to me of his exploits in World War 2. However, only when he reached the age of 76, soon after my dear mother Ruth passed away, did he express the wish that his experiences should be published.

It is indicative of his fine character that Dad never boasted of his military acts and achievements. Nor did he complain of the horrendous hardships which he endured.

While I was on a visit to South Africa, to celebrate Dad's 95th birthday, in January 2015, he was still amazingly active and alert. We resolved that this unique tale of his youth, his military experiences, and his re-entry into civilian life, should be recorded for publication. We had pondered over this possibility for almost twenty years, but my circumstances and pressure of work had delayed the matter.

I compiled and wrote this account, with the help and support of several other people. I took responsibility for further research, and I designed all of the layout and cover graphics.

The bulk of the content relating to the Second World War comes from the following sources:
Firstly, Dad and I spent many long intensive hours in Johannesburg, with him relating his military and life story to me. There were many instances during those sessions when Dad's long-term memory kicked in, and he started to recall details that had escaped from his memory for well over half a century.

When I was back in Ireland, Dad and I spent many hours on the phone, discussing the subject matter of this book. In June 2015, I returned to South Africa for a month, to complete the research for this task. Dad's short-term memory was then fading. However whilst he was forgetting recent situations and experiencing some confusion, his recall of events from his boyhood, up until a few years ago, was unbelievably detailed.

Secondly Dad had a personal journal, which he had handwritten with terrific literary skill, while he was on recuperation leave, having been honourably discharged from the army after returning to South Africa, in 1944.

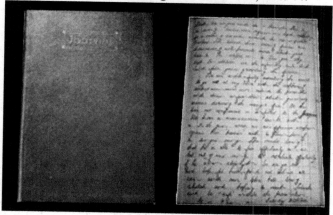

Stan's Journal

Thirdly, Dad retained a massive amount of documentation, articles, correspondence, maps and photographs, in English and Italian, which I have been privileged to utilize.

Fourthly, an exceptionally helpful source was excerpts from some fine journalism about Dad, by David Saks, over the last decade, in the South African Jewish media.
David spent many hours interviewing Dad and writing about him over the years. David joined the South African Jewish Board of Deputies (SAJBD) as Senior Researcher

in April 1997, and was appointed Associate Director in 2005. He has been editor of the Board's journal *Jewish Affairs* since 1999, and he is a regular contributor to the SA Jewish Report and other Jewish publications.

David Saks

Significantly, prior to joining the Board, David was Curator of History at Museum Africa. He holds an M.A. in History from Rhodes University. Thus, I was privileged and delighted to have him on board, to edit the military aspects of the book. I found his knowledge and insight into this subject matter to be invaluable.

David is also an author in his own right, and in his book *Boerejode – Jews in the Boer Armed Forces, 1899-1902,* he features at some length Jeanott (John) Weinberg, an uncle of Dad's, who fought for the Boers during the Anglo-Boer War, and who himself became a POW, in Ceylon.

My dear wife, Natasha, has not only given her support, but her wholehearted backing of this project, which has taken me far from home for many months, and involved me working late into the night, for prolonged periods.

Sadly, in February 2015, Natasha's father Raymond Daniel passed away, after thirteen years of blindness. He was only 75 at the time. He and I had developed a brotherly bond and a very close friendship. In the almost 20 years that we knew each other, a cross word never passed between us. I was privileged to speak at his memorial service. He had a very warm respect for Dad, and encouraged me to write this book. Natasha's mom Rika, though still in mourning, gave me great inspiration and support while I was completing this book.

Natasha & Jeff Smollan August 2002

STAN SMOLLAN
ENLISTS

1939
WAR IS DECLARED
AGAINST GERMANY

1 September 1939
At dawn on 1 September 1939, German troops stormed across the Polish frontier. A little over an hour later Nazi dive-bombers were attacking the civilians of Poland's capital city Warsaw.

1 September 1939
At 10:00 Hitler addressed the Reichstag. He said he had negotiated a settlement with the Poles, but they had refused his offers.

11:00 3 September 1939
At 09:00 on the morning of 3 September,the British Ambassador in Berlin presented an ultimatum to Hitler demanding he respond in two hours.

No answer was received…..

Stan Smollan

Escape To Anzio

On 1st September 1939, the forces of Nazi Germany launched a massive surprise assault on neighbouring Poland. Two days later, Britain and France declared war on Germany, thereby beginning what came to be known as the Second World War (WWII).

On 6th September 1939 South Africa followed suit. Before long, tens of thousands of young men began flocking to recruitment stations around the country. Some 340,000 South African men and women ultimately served in the Union Defence Force, the armed forces of the then Union of South Africa. They served, inter alia, in Madagascar, and in the North African, East African and Italian theatres of World War II.

On 13th July 1940, at the age of 20, Stan Smollan presented himself at the Drill Hall and joined up with the Second Battalion of the Transvaal Scottish Regiment. The corner-stone of the Drill Hall in Johannesburg was unveiled on 11th June 1904 by Lieutenant-General Sir H.J.T. Hildyard, Commander of the British forces in South Africa. The building was erected on the site of an old prison. It was the headquarters of the Transvaal Volunteer Corps. At the end of the Anglo-Boer War, units incorporated into the Transvaal Volunteer Corps included the Transvaal Scottish Volunteers. The Drill Hall is now a national monument.

By joining up, Stan became one of some 9400 young Jewish men, out of a South African Jewish population of around a hundred thousand, who ultimately served in the South African armed forces during WWII.

The Transvaal Scottish Regiment was established shortly after the conclusion of the Anglo-Boer War, in 1902. Its initial membership consisted of recently demobilized soldiers from the various Scottish regiments, who had fought against the Boers. However, in 1940, a '*Jock*' as members of the Transvaal Scottish are known, was as likely to be named 'Pienaar' or 'Cohen' (or 'Smollan' for that matter) as 'MacDonald'.

Most of the regiment's battle honours since its establishment had been acquired in putting down local uprisings – the 1906 Bambatha Rebellion in Natal, the 1914 Afrikaner Rebellion and, most notably, the 1922 Rand Revolt between South African government forces and striking miners in and around Johannesburg. Here the regiment sustained nearly a hundred casualties.

The Transvaal Scottish had also taken part in the conquest of German South West Africa in 1915, in the early part of WWI.

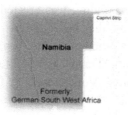

Now the Transvaal Scottish Regiment was going to be making its presence felt on the international stage for the first time.

MILITARY TRAINING

&

JOURNEY TO EGYPT

Stan and his companion volunteers had brief initial training at the Union Grounds, opposite the Drill Hall in Johannesburg, and then commenced further training in Barberton, in what at the time was known as the Eastern Transvaal, in today's Mpumalanga Province. He and his fellow young trainees were then moved for further training to Rifle Range Road, Mondeor, Johannesburg South. Thereafter they were transferred to Zonderwater, near the township of Cullinan, north-east of Pretoria.

Men of the South African Armoured Division arrive at Cullinan Train Station for training at the new military base. Source: http://samilitaryhistory.org/vol141jl.html

Zonderwater was to become the site for the largest Prisoner of War camp to be operated by the entire Allied forces, during the Second World War.

It was in this area that the famous Cullinan Diamond, at over four inches long, and weighing more than three thousand carat, the largest gem-quality diamond ever discovered, was found on 26 January 1905, in the Premier No. 2 mine.

Cullinan Diamond
Photo: Wikipedia

On completion of training, the regiment was transferred to Oribi Camp in Pietermaritzburg, Natal. The lads slept in bell tents, eight men to a tent. Pietermaritzburg is bitterly cold in winter, so the experience was "far from pleasant".

In May 1941, the entire Second Division of the Union Defence Force boarded trains at Oribi Station, and travelled by rail directly to the embarkation site in Durban.

The soldiers boarded three massive trans-atlantic liners, which had been converted into fully armed troop ships - *Nieuw Amsterdam, SS Île de France* and *HMT Mauretania.*

Nieuw Amsterdam was a Dutch ocean liner, built in Rotterdam. She was cruising the Caribbean Sea during May 1940, when the Germans occupied neutral Holland.

Nieuw-Amsterdam.   Photo: Holland America Line
http://www.hollandamericablog.com/holland-line-ships-
past-and-present/the-nieuw-amsterdam-ii-of-1938/

The ship immediately steamed for New York, and its owners decided to place the vessel under British authority. It then sailed to Halifax, where its luxury fittings were removed, for conversion to a troop ship. Because of its above average capacity for speed, this ship often sailed solo, and seldom in convoy. It was the second of three Holland America ships with that name, and is considered by many to have been Holland America's finest ship. From 1940 to 1946, she carried 378 361 soldiers, over a distance of over half a million miles. This represented an average of almost eight and a half thousand passengers on forty-four voyages, of over twelve thousand miles each!

The second ship was the *SS Île de France*. The three-funnelled Ile de France had tied up alongside the Charl Malan Quay in Port Elizabeth, during one of her visits to the city.

SS Ile de France c1935 (from picture post card)

She was subjected to one of the less happy events to befall this magnificent ship. Furniture, chandeliers, carpets, fittings, all the evidences of her former luxury, including hundreds of square feet of rare and beautiful panelling, were ruthlessly torn out and flung on the quayside, as she was completely gutted for use as a troopship.

Stan boarded the *HMT Mauretania*, which sailed in convoy with the other two liners.

Mauretania (postcard picture)

The ship travelled over half a million miles and transported almost three hundred and fifty thousand troops during the Second World War, sailing on the 'Suez Shuttle' – from Bombay to Colombo to Durban and the up to Port Tewfik (or Taufiq), opposite Suez. She made this arduous route from mid-1941 until February 1943, carrying an average of six and a half thousand men at a time

Escape To Anzio

Stan recalled:

"Each ship contained several thousand men. Ordinary soldiers, like myself, slept in hammocks on the promenade decks.

On entering the Red Sea, I remember, that we saw the longest beach we had ever seen. It was Arabia! We arrived in due course at Tewfik (or Taufiq) at the head of the Gulf of Suez. There, we disembarked in baskets, which were lowered onto barges to take us to land. There was no harbour."

NORTH AFRICA

The troops' destination was North Africa's Western Desert, where for the previous eight months a fierce battle for supremacy, between the British Eighth Army on the one hand, and German and Italian forces on the other, had been underway. The battlegrounds were spread along the coastal and adjacent inland regions of Egypt. It was by then independent of British rule, but still a region where many British troops were based, to protect the Suez Canal and also Libya, at the time still an Italian colony. The Eighth Army largely comprised Colonial and Dominion units, including divisions from Australia, New Zealand and India and with two South African divisions to come. The campaign had begun the previous December, with a devastatingly successful counter-offensive, that had hurled the invading Italians out of Egypt, and was followed up with a deep push into Libya.

However, things changed rapidly with the arrival of Colonel-General Erwin Rommel and the first units of his Deutsche Afrika Korps in February 1941.

Erwin Johannes Eugen Rommel (15 Nov. 1891 – 14 Oct. 1944), was a German Field Marshall of World War II. He earned the respect of both his own troops and his enemies. Rommel was a highly decorated officer in World War I, and was awarded the "Pour le Mérite" for his exploits on the Italian Front. In World War II, he further distinguished himself as the commander of the 7th Panzer Division, during the 1940 invasion of France. His leadership of German and Italian forces in the North African campaign established him as one of the most able commanders of the war, and earned him the appellation of the "Desert Fox" - Wüstenfuchs, because he was regarded as one of the most skilled commanders of desert warfare in the conflict.

Field Marshall Erwin Rommel
(Picture Wikipeadia)

He later commanded the German forces opposing the Allied cross-channel invasion of Normandy. His assignments never took him to the Eastern Front.

Rommel is regarded as having been a civilized and professional officer. His Afrika Korps was never accused of war crimes, and Allied soldiers captured during his Africa campaign were reported to have been treated humanely.

Orders to kill Jewish soldiers, civilians and captured commandos were ignored by Rommel.

Later in the war, he was linked to the conspiracy to assassinate Adolf Hitler. Because Rommel was a national hero, Hitler desired to eliminate him quietly. He forced Rommel to commit suicide with a cyanide pill, in return for assurances that Rommel's family would not be persecuted following his death. He was given a state funeral, and it was announced that Rommel had succumbed to his injuries from an earlier strafing of his staff car in Normandy.

Extract from Wikipedia.

Through his energy, daring and tactical genius, Rommel had his opponents on the back foot for the greater part of the next two years. Eventually numerical superiority, together with the gritty professionalism of their new Commander-in-Chief Lieutenant-General Bernard Montgomery, saw the British and Commonwealth forces come out on top in the Egypt-Libya theatre, and once American forces began to arrive, the Axis defeat in North Africa was only a matter of time. By then, however, over ten thousand South Africans had been kicking their heels in a succession of prisoner of war camps for over a year.

By the end of April, Rommel had regained the initiative in Libya, by regaining most of the captured territory with the exception of the port city of Tobruk, a fateful name in the annals of South African military history. As will be described later in this account, Tobruk was being subjected to what would become an eight-month siege, which lasted until December 1941, when it was finally lifted during the so-called Operation Crusader.

This was the state of play in May 1941, when the Second South African Division (Stan Smollan included) set out from Durban and sailed up the East Coast of Africa.

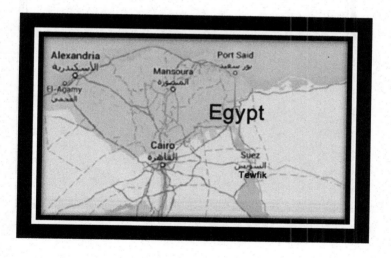

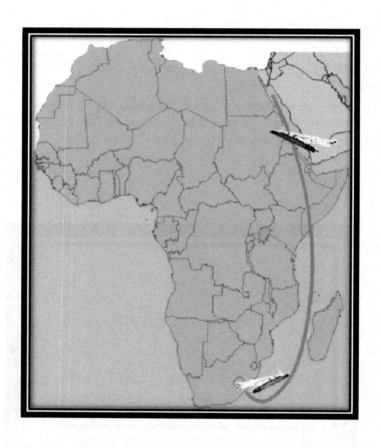

The men were brought from Tewfik by road to a barracks called 'Mariobolis', where they remained for approximately a month. Thereafter they were loaded onto cattle trucks, to be transported by rail up to the north coast of Egypt. Disembarking from the train, all they could see was a hut and a long sign with the name "Ël Alamein". El Alamein, located on the Mediterranean coast about 140 km west of Alexandria, was at the time still an obscure desert village. None of these men could have reasonably predicted that Ël Alamein was to become one of the most famous battle sites in history!

Stan Smollan, El Alamein – with other
soldiers from his regiment

The Second Transvaal Scottish Battalion, together with two battalions from the South African Police, made up the Sixth South African Infantry Brigade, whose assignment was to help prepare the defenses. Their daily task was to hack trenches out of the desert rock, from inland to the coast. They came to realise (fuelled by rumours) that this was the last line of defense, where the desert war could be won or lost.

The First South African Division was part of the team that wired and mined the now famous "Alamein Box", a large secured area surrounded by minefields and barbed wire, around the railway station at El Alamein on the coast. This was the first and strongest 'box' to be built by the Allies. In later years, when Stan read the historical accounts of the period, it became obvious to him that very few people knew that the battle at El Alamein was fought on a short line of under two miles."

Qattara Depression

Here there was a huge depressed area called The Qattara Depression, which contains the second lowest point in Africa at 436 feet below sea level (the lowest being Lake Assal in Djibouti, on the Horn of Africa.) The impassable Qattara Depression covers over seven and a half thousand square miles, and would prevent any possible chance of being outflanked by the enemy, because no truck or man would possibly survive in this vast, merciless wasteland.

In Stan's opinion the Western Desert Campaign was fought like a naval battle "Open spaces with no distractions."

After leaving El Alamein, the regiment was involved in two military actions. One was at Fort Capuzza, located in Libya a little inland, and the other at nearby Sollum, a fortified coastal village on the Egyptian side of the border. Sollum had already been the scene of heavy fighting the previous year. The action involving the Second Transvaal Scottish Battalion is sometimes referred to as *The Battle of Clayden's Trench*.

On 11 January 1942, a day after Stan's 22nd birthday, the Sixth South African Infantry Brigade fought in the assault on Sollum.

The attack was part of Operation Battleaxe, which was a British operation, aimed at clearing eastern Cyrenaica of German and Italian forces.

Escape To Anzio

South African soldiers at Sollum in January 1942 attacking a machine gun nest, equipped with grenades and Enfield rifles.

The Brigade went on to fight in the battles of Bardia, Acroma Keep and Gazala. At Bardia, Sollum and Halfaya, both German and Italian troops were forced to surrender.

Carel Birkby, a war correspondent at Sollum, wrote: *"The sand storm died down during the night while the men moved forward in the chill that struck to the marrow.*

Moving down on to the narrow plain where Sollum lies were men of a South African Scottish Battalion, who were going into serious battle for the first time.

The action began at 06h40 - the Scottish platoons moving on Sollum itself, had a harder and more spectacular fight. From the heights we could see the bursts of high-explosive shells and shrapnel, and the brief bursts of mortar-bombs all over the wadi (valley), towards the shell-riven houses that make up Sollum. The rattle of machine-gun fire came softly up the escarpment. Check and advance, check and advance. Thus they cleared up nests of enemy resistance.

Far away to the left another column of Springboks were fighting their way forward. They were clearing trenches and dugouts and caves on the coast where enemy sections tried in vain to hold out. They forced their way through Sollum itself and out along a narrow spit of land to a pier. They cleared the pier. They had 40 prisoners - now machine-guns opened from a cave they had passed by - then the Germans dragged forward mortars and began to pump bombs at them.

Some desperate fighting went on around that tongue of land and the cape just beyond Sollum after this. Our infantry judiciously waited for reinforcements. The South African artillery up on the escarpment - actually in Libya and firing across the border into Egypt - laid down a barrage on the enemy. The German 75s at Halfaya Pass opened up at the same time. Two separate, shifting rows of shellbursts showed up on the plain down there and from a distance it all seemed curiously unreal. Yet here was one link with reality, one reminder that actual battle was in progress there below. Two dot-like figures were slowly moving in a wadi. I focused my field-glasses on them. One was a Jock rifleman, and the other a wounded comrade whom he was helping slowly over the rocks and sandy patches of the watercourse. Grey puffs nearby told of enemy mortar bombs exploding round them."

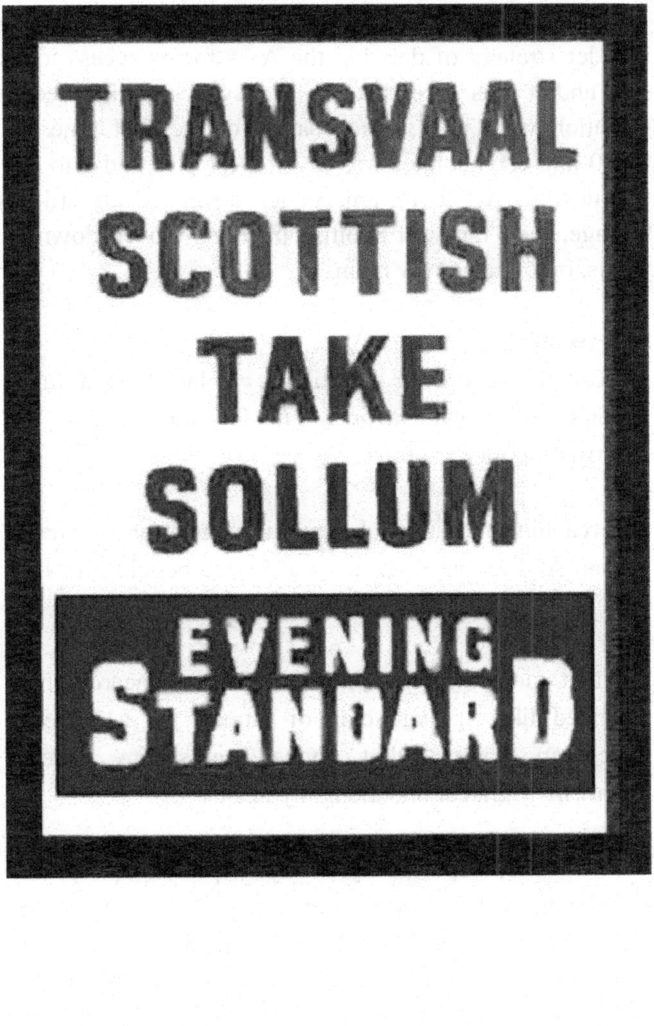
TRANSVAAL
SCOTTISH
TAKE
SOLLUM
EVENING
STANDARD

WOUNDED IN BATTLE

The dawn attack on the Italians at Sollum was part of a broader strategy of denying the Axis forces access to the sea, and it was here that the Transvaal Scottish Second Battalion went into serious battle for the first time. At 04.00 am, each soldier was given a tot of brandy, to cool the nerves. At 06.40 am, under cover of an artillery barrage, the Transvaal Scottish platoons moved down the wadis, onto the narrow plain.

Stan recalled:

"Close to the enemy positions, we launched a full-frontal regimental bayonet run for forty yards, to overrun the forward lines.

On reaching the target, I came up against an unarmed Italian soldier, on his hands and knees, begging for his life. **I chose not to shoot!**

At that moment, I turned my head, and heard what sounded like 'a huge clap of thunder' as a sniper's incendiary tracer bullet scythed across my cheek, below my right ear and along my neck.

As has been reported by many a person in fear of imminent death, I saw my life passing before me like a film. Dazed and bleeding, I needed medical attention. I was one of over a hundred Transvaal Scottish casualties incurred during that successful operation. They included one of my very close friends, John Mendelsohn, who was killed in action, and another friend, Phillip Medalie, who was so seriously wounded, that he would spend the rest of his life in a wheelchair."

Stan later found himself on a fully marked 1914 hospital ship in Tobruk. He was bandaged with a field dressing and his scarf. Some surgery was performed on the decks.

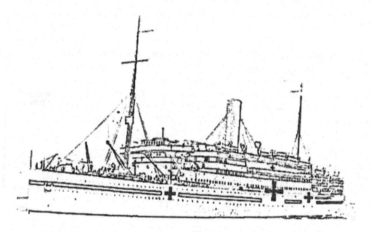

He eventually went by rail via Alexandria to the Fifth General Hospital, at Rosetta, Cairo, which was at that time the largest hospital in the Middle East.

T. 27. POST OFFICE TELEGRAPHS.—POSKANTOORTELEGRAAFDIENS.

| PJ49 | GOVT | PRETORIA | 45/44 | 5/20PM | | |

MR M SMOLLAN KILLARNEY COURT KILLARNEY
JOHANNESBURG

WRC 79/3650. DEPARTMENT OF DEFENCE REGRETS TO INFORM
YOU THAT YOUR SON NO 27498 PRIVATE STANLEY SOLOMON
SMOLLAN IS REPORTED WOUNDED IN ACTION ADDRESSED MR M
SMOLLAN KILLARNEY COURT KILLARNEY JOHANNESBURG REPEATED
MAGISTRATE JOHANNESBURG DEWAREC +

2 79/3650 27498 +

Telegrams received by Moss Smollan, regarding his son,
Private Stanley Smollan

T. 27. POST OFFICE TELEGRAPHS.—POSKANTOORTELEGRAAFDIENS.

| PJA | 446 | G PRETORIA | 37/35 | 3/32PM | | |

MR M SMOLLAN 009 KILLARNEY COURT KILLARNEY JHBURG

+ WRC 79/3650 FURTHER TO TELEGRAM 23/1/42 DEPARTMENT OF DEFENCE

WISHES TO INFORM YOU THAT YOUR SON NO 27498 PRIVATE STANLEY SOLOMON

SUSTAINED GUNSHOT WOUNDS RIGHT CHEEK + DEWAREC

+ 009 79/3650 23/1/42 27498

Stan's cousin Fred Smollan also served in the war. He was a commissioned officer, having attained the rank of lieutenant in the Imperial Light Horse Regiment, nicknamed the "*Aikona, No Horse Regiment*" ("Aikona" is a Nguni expression of disbelief widely used in Southern Africa). Upon hearing of Stan's injuries, Fred visited Stan, who also later saw him in his officer's quarters. Fred was a former Rugby Springbok, who had played for South Africa against Australia in 1933 alongside his great friend Doctor Danie Craven, *Mr Rugby*, who not only created the physical training division of the Union Defence Force (1941), but also later became the first Professor of Physical Education at Stellenbosch University. Stan was later to meet "Doc" Dr. Craven in his Rehabilitation Gymnasium.

Fred Smollan.
Wikipedia

Danie Craven.
Wikipedia

The Fifth General Hospital was in a very lush part of Egypt. While recuperating, Stan and some of his comrades went to Alexandria, where they were accommodated in a home which the Alexander family had given over to the war effort. The patients visited Stanley Bay and were invited out to dinner by some of the locals, who were exceptionally hospitable.

Stan Smollan, outside The Jewish Club in Cairo, March 1941, while recuperating from a facial gunshot injury sustained at Sollum,

Outside the Jewish Club in Cairo- Herby Justus,
Jim Kinnear and Stanley Smollan

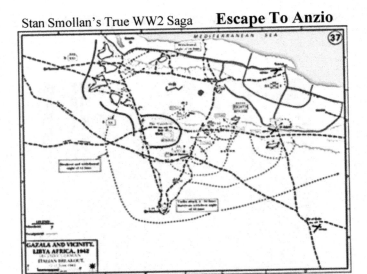

Image: Wikipedia

Bundesarchiv_Bild_101I-785-0294-
32A,_Tobruk,_englische_Kriegsgefangene

REJOINING THE REGIMENT IN TOBRUK

Three months after being wounded at Sollum, Stan was discharged from the hospital in Cairo, having recovered from his wounds. On the 15th June 1942, he was drafted back to the Transvaal Scottish Second Battalion, and seven days later, on the 22nd June 1942, he arrived in Tobruk, where he rejoined his regiment.

The timing could not have been worse!

In the weeks prior to Stan's return to the front, Rommel and his Eighth Army counterpart Lieutenant-General Neil Ritchie (under the overall authority of the Commander-in-Chief Middle East, General Sir Claude Auchinleck), had been engaged in an extended series of actions that is now generally referred to as the Battle of Gazala (26 May – 21 June 1942). By the middle of June, the British were in precipitous retreat, having been thoroughly outfought and outgeneraled by the 'Desert Fox' and his Panzer Army. In a series of hard-fought engagements, Rommel had succeeded in driving around the southern flank of the Gazala line, overrunning key positions and forcing the badly mauled Eighth Army units, British, Free French, South African and Indian, to fall back on the Egyptian frontier to avoid encirclement.

Even worse, the Tobruk garrison was now left high and dry, cut off from all hope of timely relief. It was hoped that the fortress would once again be able to withstand a prolonged siege. Rommel, however, had other ideas.

At dawn on 20th June, the day that Stan arrived, Rommel attacked from the south-east with his two Panzer divisions and the Italian XX Corps. Meanwhile, the fearsome Stuka dive-bombers were screaming down continually, raining death and destruction on the hard-pressed defenders. By midday, the defensive antitank ditch had been bridged, and exploiting the breach, the German and Italian heavy artillery were soon pounding the ships in the harbour.

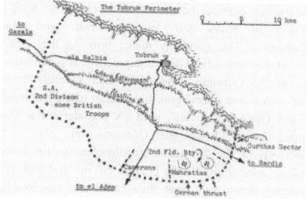

This hand-drawn map by H A Candy shows the desperate situation faced by the 2nd Field Battery as a result of the German penetration of the south-east perimeter of the Tobruk defences.

By that evening, the strategically vital Solaro and Pilastrano forts to the west had fallen to the 21st Panzer Division.

The western perimeter of Tobruk, where Stan and his comrade soldiers were positioned, comprised a string of barbed wire defences, extending for a radius of twenty miles around the all-important harbour.

In between the series of fences, there were literally thousands of anti-personnel mines, which merely had to be stepped on, to blow a soldier to smithereens! In addition, infantry, tanks and field guns were guarding the fortress.

Stan was one of a group of mobile infantry awaiting the word to go outside the perimeter, at any time, with the support of tanks and armoured cars, and obtain information. This generally meant drawing the enemy's fire. At this time, the Allied equipment was far inferior to that of the Germans. The Allies had a reconnaissance tank with a two pound gun, used as an offensive weapon against German 'heavies', with six pounders of a longer range. The result was that Germans were able to fire effectively on the defenders, but out of range for them to retaliate adequately. So the chaps went out and looked for Germans, found out what they could and ran like hell, being shelled and hoping to reach Tobruk and be 'safe' inside the perimeter.

Stan later wrote in his journal: *"It was 9.00 am on Saturday, 20th June, 1942. We were having our breakfast, about three hundred yards off the coastal road to Derna, which was barely inside of the western perimeter. A tremendous artillery barrage now opened up on the road, forcing us to dive for cover into slit trenches. These were just wide enough and long enough to hold a man lying flat, and provide cover from shrapnel and blast, if he did not get a direct hit!*

This carried on until an order went out to "man defences on the west". The Germans had broken through the East Wire, but our forces had counter attacked, and consolidated their positions.

For three days now, we have been the new beleaguered Garrison of Tobruk, and we are going to hold on to it for months if necessary said an order of the day. So, we got into our trucks and moved, knowing full well that the enemy's observer could see us.

Everyone is tense just waiting for the shell to arrive. However, we continued and reached our destination, right on the outer western wire defences. We knew that things had gone wrong. German Messerschmitt fighter aircraft blackened the sky in waves of about thirty, one wave after another, all the time unopposed.

The British aerodromes at El Aden were lost. We even watched the enemy taking off to blow our minefields and our comrades to pieces, and to make gaps in the lines, through which infantry and tanks could pour in. We witnessed a patterned low flying strafing of the entire minefield from east to west. This set up a cloud of smoke over Tobruk which lasted many days."

Private G D van Zyl, of the 1st South African Police Regiment, later aptly characterised the men of the Second South African Division during the battle of Tobruk as "sheep without a shepherd".

Ike Rosmarin, a war correspondent with the Division, described the attack as: "terrifying [but] worst of all, was the fact that we did not know what was happening, as there were no orders from our officers. Confusion reigned with fear and panic".

South African soldier taking cover during
an Air Attack

Having no clear orders was bad enough, but receiving conflicting orders was even worse. Assailed from all directions by superior forces, the men did not know whether they were expected to hold their ground, destroy their weapons and try to escape, or to make their way to the coast to await evacuation. There was tension and confusion during those last chaotic hours before the surrender:

At 5.30pm on the 20th June 1942, a British officer arrived on the scene, saying that the ferry was in the harbour (15 miles east of the men). He was going to bury his transport,

and make an attempt on foot to pass through the wire and
rejoin the retreating Allied armies.

This was a huge shock to Stan and his fellow soldiers! The
men's last order had been to "man the wire" and that they
absolutely had to stop the breakthrough. A lieutenant
phoned company headquarters. The order he received was
to fight to the last man and to the last round, until 12
o'clock on that Sunday, when it was hoped that an Allied
striking force would reach them from Mersa Matruh, a
Mediterranean seaport on the Egyptian coast.

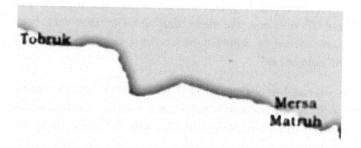

MAJOR-GENERAL KLOPPER SURRENDERS TOBRUK TO AXIS FORCES

After the war
Winston Churchill wrote in his book
The Second World War:
"This is one of the heaviest blows I can recall
during the war."

THE ALLIES
SURRENDER TOBRUK

Stan wrote in his journal:
"We prepare for Death or Glory and all of us are tense all night. Everyone thinks he sees figures moving in the dark, on the other side of the wire, but thankfully, as first light comes, nothing happens, and all is peaceful with the sun up. Then comes the news that the Garrison had been surrendered on Saturday night. Burn transport, guns and all equipment!"

So far as Major-General H B Klopper was concerned, the position had become hopeless, and to resist further, would lead to further futile loss of life, with the result being the same in the end.

Therefore, at 09h40 on 21st June, 1942, he surrendered the garrison to General Enea Navarrini.

At a stroke, the entire South African Second Division of 10,722 men and some 25,000 other Allied troops became prisoners of war. They had lost more than 2,000 vehicles, 2,000 tons of fuel, and 5,000 tons of rations. Far from "holding out for months", the defence by Tobruk's "beleaguered garrison" had barely lasted four days!

Major-General H B Klopper (Wikipedia)

Stan later wrote in his journal:

"We entered into Tobruk only to be part of a general surrender by Major-General Klopper. Our particular platoon was right on the western perimeter, and we saw the frightful saturated Stuka bombings of all the outer defences, designed to eradicate any minefields laid by previous regiments. This caused a pall of smoke, which would last for days, and be visible for miles. There was very little left inside. In my opinion, it was a hopeless situation. General Klopper was

*severely criticized [for surrendering] but really there
was nothing there. It would have been a massacre".*

In 1943, General Klopper himself escaped from captivity,
and he was subsequently unconditionally exonerated for
the course of action he took over Tobruk. After the war,
Klopper attained the rank of Commandant-General. This
made him head of the South African Union Defence Force
from 1956 to 1958.

It may have been true that Tobruk had withstood a lengthy
siege the previous year, but so costly had it been to
maintain its defence, that the British Middle East High
Command had since decided that the position would never
again be held in isolation. As a result, its defences had
been allowed to become dangerously derelict, making it
relatively easy for the Germans to break through. On
reflection, the Tobruk garrison should have been
evacuated days before, along with the other defeated units
of the Eighth Army that had withdrawn across the border.
Instead, Major-General Klopper had been left in an
indefensible position. He had insufficient anti-aircraft and
anti-tank guns, and he was expected somehow to fight it
out.

Inside Tobruk a major logistical problem arose for the
commander, General Klopper, as to how to evacuate some
30,000 troops whose destination was to be Benghazi, at
the time still a small village.

Stan recalled: *"I was on the outer edge of the British
position. Cyril Cunningham, Vic Harding, and myself*

decided to attempt to escape, after hearing of the surrender. Some of the Transvaal Scottish broke up into small parties, and tried to make their way deeper into the desert, to evade their captors. The only hope for those who wished it was to cross the minefields, get into the desert, and try to walk in the direction of the Allied troops.

I did this with my two companions. After half an hour of nerve-racking tiptoeing through minefields, expecting concealed mines to blowup under us at any moment, we were suddenly through the wire!"

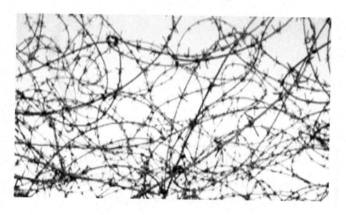

DEPARTMENT OF DEFENSE
REGRETS TO INFORM YOU
THAT YOUR SON 27498 PRIVATE
STANLEY SOLOMON SMOLLAN
REPORTED MISSING 20 JUNE

CAPTURE

"Now the intention was to try to get well into the desert, and from there make our way to the British lines on the Egyptian side of the border. We each carried a quart of water, and little food. We wore shirts and shorts. We foolishly made no provision for possible capture, or the approaching bitter winter. We walked for about half a day, but in the end we were spotted and picked up by patrolling Italian motor cyclists who, out-numbering us, took us without trouble or resistance.

Photograph: afrikakorps.forumcrea.com

After we were taken prisoner, the chaps and I found ourselves in a pretty awkward position. We were handed over to a German patrol, whose officer addressed us as follows: *"Gentlemen, you are my prisoners. I have just enjoyed some of your wonderful fruits and jams, from your stores, which we have captured.*

I remember how the officer, on learning that we were South Africans, asked us, Why don't you do what the Irish do. Join us and tell Britain where to get off? Of course, the chaps could only reply that they would find this rather difficult to do. The German officer continued: Look chaps, I am now going to say farewell, and I apologize for handing you over to the Italians, who you had in the last war and we have in this war."

He did precisely that. I remember the genuine mutual respect that existed between Rommel's German troops and the British and American soldiers who opposed them. However the same was not true with regard to the Italians, who appear not to have been fully respected by their German allies. The Afrika Korps officer's clearly disdainful attitude towards the Italian military, is apparently mirrored by remarks made by none other than Colonel-General Erwin Rommel himself."

According to Bernard Schwikkard of the 3rd Transvaal Scottish, when he and his group were captured:
"General Rommel, the famous German Commander, drove up to us and said he was sorry to be handing us

over to the Italians, but he needed all his soldiers to do the fighting. He indicated that as soldiers, the Italians were somewhat questionably looked upon".

It is interesting to record that Rommel was so highly regarded by the rank-and-file Allied troops, that the latter's senior officers are alleged to have been instructed to refer in their communications simply to "the enemy", since referring to Rommel by name was bad for morale. After the capture of Tobruk, the high point of his career, Rommel was promoted to Field Marshall.

The prisoners' morale, as can be imagined, was pretty low. They were tired, thirsty and hungry. They started to imagine what was in store for them. . . . ***Perhaps years!***

They had to walk some twelve miles into an area of less than an acre, where some six thousand men were herded like cattle. Some Italians jeered at the prisoners and made vulgar gesticulations. The prisoners' thirst was maddening. At that time of the year on the Libyan coastline, one finds it torturous to keep away from a water bottle for more than an hour. After six hours, the men were sent a single drum of water. Some gangster elements amongst the prisoners rushed the drum, and in the mad resultant dogfight, half of the precious liquid was spilled on the ground. Stan said that only those with the least self-respect and conscience got to drink. Eventually the Italians agreed to provide four gallons of water for every thirty men. That amounted to barely a pint (about half a litre) of water per man.

Once again, a dogfight unfolded. It was stopped by a magnificent example of the discipline of the Coldstream Guards, part of the Foot Guards Division, of the British Army. One of the oldest regiments in the Regular British Army, it originated in Coldstream, Scotland, in 1650 and had been in continuous active service since then. While the fight for water was on, a sergeant in the Guards rapped out Guardsmen fall in! There was an immediate response, in that from nowhere, more than fifty Guardsmen had fallen in, in columns of threes. This had a sobering effect on the rest of the men. Thanks to this demonstration of restraint and discipline, all the men lined up, and each man got a meager ration of half a cup of water.

Stan recounted: *"While this was going on, a German officer came up and asked me which battalion of the Transvaal Scottish I was in, as he had noticed the headdress. I told him that I was not entitled to tell him. The officer very decently asked me over to his tent, and gave me water. He apologized profusely that he had no food to offer. He then sympathized, that after we had fought so magnificently against them (the Germans), we had to be prisoners of the Italians. He said that they thought as much of the Italians, as the Russians thought of the English (which was, I thought, a rather a nasty crack!). He asked me about South Africa, commenting that he thought it was a great pity that the country had not remained neutral, since now they (the Germans) would take Cairo, and then sweep south to the Cape.*

He left me, saying that he was off east to Cairo, and that he too might be a prisoner within a few days. To this I rejoined, "I hope that I will be as well treated by the Italians as you will be by us."

We were able to see that these Germans were not the so-called "Nazi Death or Glory boys", but perfectly normal human beings, who gave us all the respect that was befitting soldiers who had lost fighting. Some Italians on the other hand, attempted to degrade us with jeering and gesticulations.

I later learned that one of the Company Commanders of the Transvaal Scottish, Captain Paddy Cook and his companions had also tried to escape at Tobruk, and that they had made it in the end. They went right into the desert, caught up with the 'Desert Rats' and got back to Cairo.

A Black African soldier also made it, and he was later decorated. However, not many others were successful."

The Desert Rats were the Seventh Armoured Division of the British Army. They saw active service during World War II, when their exploits made them famous. On 4th November 1942, a little over four months after the low-point of the Gazala defeat and the fall of Tobruk, they took part in the Battle of El Alamein, the British victory that turned the tide of the war in North Africa. Historians later revealed that Montgomery had disobeyed Churchill's order to attack 'immediately' and chose rather to wait for the American Sherman tanks who, as he predicted, provided him with the superiority in men and material that he needed to defeat Rommel's Panzer Army, and set the Germans in full flight. Monty (Field Marshall Montgomery) had strategically used the area between the Qattara Depression and the sea, to the Allies' advantage.

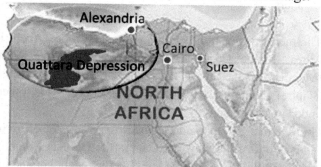

The South African 1st Division was likewise involved in the victory, which Winston Churchill famously described at the time, as being for the greater Allied cause, *"not the beginning of the end, but the end of the beginning"*.

However, those taken prisoner at Tobruk would only learn piece-meal about all of this in the long months of captivity to come. Cut off from all news from the outside world, their focus was now simply on surviving the experience of confinement, and finding ways to make day-to-day living conditions more bearable.

The captives were taken on large trucks, similar to cattle trucks, for almost 300 miles (480 km) west to Benghazi, along a coastal road via Derna.

There a camp had been hastily constructed. Unfortunately, things deteriorated very rapidly thereafter, and the situation in the camp was soon reduced to one of near anarchy. Eventually a Transvaal Scottish Sergeant Major Cockcroft, together with a Guards Officer, took charge of things, restored a degree of order, and the situation improved slightly, but it was still very grim for the prisoners.

The men's destination was soon revealed to be Tripoli, in Libya. Major Cockroft was later awarded an MBE (Member of the Most Excellent Order of the British Empire). Some prisoners arrived in Greece, and others ended up in Germany.
The German Command seemed to want the Tobruk captives out of the way, since they (the Germans) wanted to use Tobruk to supply the *run* that they were conducting down the desert. It was this *run* which would prove their undoing, since they over-reached themselves, and were thus decisively defeated at El Alamein.

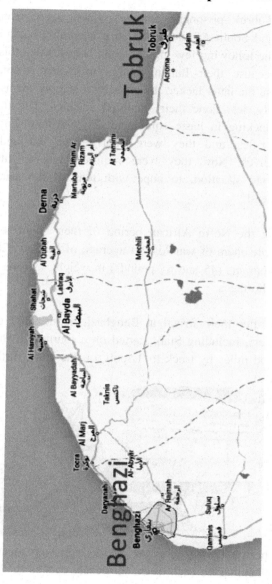

The Tobruk prisoners, amongst whom were over ten thousand South Africans, had an exceedingly harsh time, over the following few months. Stan believes that this was not because their Italian captors mistreated them, but because the latter lacked the capacity to supply themselves properly, let alone their captured enemies. The Italians were lacking in basic equipment. They were using pre-1914 rifles, and they were poorly clad and underfed themselves. Now they were required, on top of this desperate situation, to cope with tens of thousands of prisoners!

During the North African period of their confinement, most prisoners of war lost an average of between 20 and 30 kilograms (45 and 65 pounds) in weight, as a result of food shortages.

Soon after their arrival at Benghazi, about 2000 of the prisoners, including Stan, started on a journey of thirteen hundred miles by truck to Tripoli, on the coast further to the west.

The harrowing trip took ten days. There were over sixty men standing on each truck, so closely packed that it was impossible to crouch or sit. Their daily rations for the seven days were two Italian biscuits and a half a tin of very stringy meat.

At 10.00 am, they arrived at Tarhunah, a town 65 kilometres to the southeast of Tripoli, in the Murqub District. There they were confined in an old Italian barracks. Having been given meat and biscuits that morning, the captives were not fed again until 12.30 pm the following day! By that time, they were all starving and exhausted.

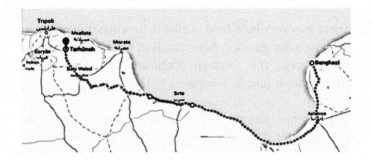

TARHUNAH

Conditions at Tarhuna proved to be no better than they had been at Benghazi. For a start, four to five thousand POWs were in premises that had been built to accommodate five hundred prisoners at most. The old cloakrooms and drainage system were not functioning, so that very quickly there was a danger of disease breaking out.

There was very little food available for either the prisoners or those who guarded them. No Red Cross support could reach them. The situation continued for a number of months, from June to November 1942.

During this period, owing to the unbelievably filthy conditions of the camps and the herding, most of the men developed serious dysentery. Many prisoners succumbed to illness during this time."

The experiences of the captured South Africans in North Africa is dealt with by the historian Dr. Karen Horn in her paper "Narratives from North Africa: South African prisoner-of-war experience following the fall of Tobruk, June 1942", (Historia vol.56, no. 2, 2011).

Amongst those who feature in Dr. Horn's paper are Stan and his friend and fellow prisoner David Brokensha. They were amongst those former POWs interviewed by Karen Horn when she was conducting research for a thesis at

Stellenbosch University. She has the following to say about the conditions the captives were subjected to:

"Many POWs consider their experiences in North African as dehumanising, referring to the camps as "cages" Maintaining a sense of dignity became a daily struggle, because living conditions worsened and. because there were so many prisoners, the distribution of food was a long process and after standing in line for hours, the POWs were always disappointed when they received their rations.

In Derna the biscuits were so hard, that Reverend Major Patrick J. Nolan asked an Italian guard to break the biscuit with his bayonet. The Italian replied that Nolan should soak the biscuit in water, but by that time the water had run out. Often POWs received tins of bully beef, but these had to be shared between two or three of them.

The shortage of food forced POWs to look for food elsewhere, and on one occasion Collet [initials GH, of the Durban Mounted Rifles] was desperate and lucky enough to catch and eat a mole."

In his diary, Stan's fellow Jock (member of the Transvaal Scottish) Dick Dickinson described the kind of food the prisoners received, and how much:

"Our daily ration is a tin of bully-beef and a small loaf of bread, the size of a large hot-cross bun, per man. The bully-beef is 300 grams. About every third day we are given a hot meal, which is a pint and a half

of stew, but which is mostly rice. When we get this meal, our bully is cut to half a tin".

The prisoners were caught up in an ugly situation. However, for most of them, their training and survival instincts kicked in. The majority of the prisoners, particularly the South Africans, conducted themselves very well. They kept themselves clean, kept their spirits up, and exercised whenever they could. It was a matter of maintaining one's self-respect and lasting out this situation. It became a strict rule, that whenever it was possible to shave or polish their boots, they should do so.

The prisoners also formed work parties of volunteers who had some knowledge of plumbing and drainage, and these volunteers were able to get things into reasonable working order. When the sewage and latrine system was reconstructed, large trenches were dug away from the actual camp. Over these trenches, poles were then placed, on which the users would sit and 'do what they had to do,' into the trench itself. There were long lines, about fifty yards or so. The rumours would start on one side and carry down to the other. This created a novel way of disseminating news that the prisoners referred to as *'latrinograms'*.

Postcard received by Stan's mother

The men were weary, sick, hungry and helpless. Nevertheless, they were considered by the Italians to be potential escapists. Not only were there inevitable, although rare, cases of abuse by guards who were put on the camp, but the strength of the barbed wire was also increased in depth, until it was eventually some fifteen feet wide. In order to carry out these preparations, the Italians obtained the services of some British and Dominion prisoners, whose stomachs meant more to them than their own freedom, or that of their unfortunate comrades. They were paid in *triple quantity rations*! Thus these men chose to sell their souls.

At night, prisoners were herded into the barrack rooms, which had concrete floors. Some got one small blanket per man. Some got none at all. Others were given one blanket to five or six men. They lay right up against each other, so tightly were they packed.

The Italian guards were mostly elderly people or retired civil servants and were kindly towards the prisoners. They were sympathetic, but they were hindered from doing anything to help the plight of the men who had dysentery. The order was that ***anyone seen outside the buildings after dark, would be shot at!*** All night, the groans of pain from dysentery, and of painful bodies on the concrete, and swearing men cursing the poor unfortunates who were attempting an excursion to the lavatories, over the bodies in the dark, would constantly be heard.

In the meantime, prisoners were in some rare cases robbed (under supervision of a few corrupt officers) of rings, watches, woollen clothing and any other valuables, most of which were foreign to the Italians. Later, the prisoners' camp leader reminded the Italians of the terms of the Geneva Convention, which forbade any such action by the detaining power.

BARTER WITH ITALIAN GUARDS

Some prisoners accepted benefits in exchange for working in the villages, which is a practise Stan refused to indulge in under any circumstances, as it was against his principles.

From then on, the Italians, who were themselves experiencing deprivation, understandably proceeded to take advantage of the prisoners, by buying or bartering articles for food or water. The rate of exchange varied from, worst case scenario, a watch for a bottle of water or two loaves of bread, or from five to fifteen Egyptian pounds for the same bread or water, up to meagre quantities of cigarettes, bread or jam for a watch. There were many thousands of Egyptian pounds in the camp. These had been brought in by the men. The money was mostly their own, and proceeds from unit canteens. In the camp, a rate of exchange was fixed at two shillings per cigarette.

The inevitable *"crown and anchor gangsters"* made their appearance. Soon large amounts fell into their hands. With this money they were able, at the expense of others, to obtain food from the sentries in exchange for Egyptian pounds. The Italian soldiers got about 300 lire a month (roughly US$25). They sold bread to the prisoners for up to two Egyptian pounds each, which they in turn sold to

Arabs for up to 400 lire each. The Arabs somehow sent these along their eighteen hundred mile camel and caravan tracks to Egypt.

Other elements in the camp bought watches and British clothing from chaps in the camp, out of their crown and anchor winnings, and in turn sold them to the enemy at great profits (of food). Therefore, while ninety per cent of the camp was starving, some of these gangsters were doing well, and it seemed to be profitable for them to degrade themselves before the enemy. . . .

It became quite common for prisoners to see an Italian sentry on his beat, fully dressed in British clothing and boots, all of which was far superior to their rags, which they had been unable to replace for years.

Now the matter of food became a major problem amongst the prisoners. It was considered and debated in the most serious terms. Some chaps became neurotic, and wrote and discussed recipes all day. Others tried all sorts of ways to make food last longer. Others hoarded and starved themselves for days, and yet others took their food and ate it, as and when it came. Some prisoners craved cigarettes, and several non-smokers took advantage of their plight, persuading them to barter their very lifeblood of a day's bread ration for a meagre ten cigarettes.

Food was dished out in strict rotation, with two sergeant majors standing at the pots, to ensure that these wild-eyed men did not come and get food twice. Catcalls were made as to whether the ladle was being filled enough. If some rice fell on the ground, then inevitably the shameless would appear and eat it off the ground. Men were appointed to carry the pots from the kitchens. For this job, their reward would be to scrape the pots. Even after this, other scavengers arrived. They were willing to carry the pots back, if the original carriers, after scraping, would allow them to clean the remnants with their fingers.

The Allied troops were eighteen hundred miles away in Egypt, and after three months, no attempt had been made to either move the prisoners to Italy, or to feed and clothe them for the coming winter. Stan and his comrades had no clue as to how long this was to be their home. Already they were lice ridden, undernourished and nerve strained.

THE POWER OF HOPE

One day, one of the ration party returned from the nearby village with amazing news, which was supposed to have originated from a British secret service party in the village. The prisoners were to organise themselves into groups. They were to exercise themselves, in case they would be required to go on a long walk. Plans were to be formulated for the overpowering of the camp guards. The effect of this *"news"* on the men was electrifying. Strained faces were replaced with smiles. The Italians were presented (much to their consternation) with the sight of the smiling although weak, and sick men, walking round and round the camp confidently. Meanwhile, the men were secretly preparing themselves for the events, which (supposedly) lay ahead.

This news appeared to be authentic, because the prisoners later learnt that it was all part of the intended surprise raid from the desert by the Long Range Desert Group, LRDG, in Benghazi and Barce, in conjunction with a sea attack on Tobruk. Unfortunately, these plans were thwarted by the enemy. Although the prisoners managed to wreak havoc, the LRDG did not succeed in rescuing them.

On the 1st of November 1942, the Italians attempted to improve conditions by putting double decker beds into the camp, and by giving each man an Italian blanket (about half the size of a British blanket). By the 15th of November, nearly five months after their capture, news began to filter through to prisoners of a withdrawal by the Axis armies. All this time, the prisoners had been fed with the most ridiculous and far-reaching rumours.

The prisoners decided to form a committee to track down the origin of every rumour, and to present these origins to the camp, as a whole. Some stouter hearts had been able to obtain Italian newspapers, by fair means and by foul. This, of course, was without the knowledge of the Italians, who would have been most concerned. The prisoners now had an admission in black and white, from the Italians' own newspapers, of their troops' withdrawal to the west. Most of the prisoners were confident of pending release. The positive spirit of the men was quite beyond the understanding of their captors.

That month, the situation had indeed changed dramatically, with the Allies defeating the Axis at El Alamein on 4th November.

The prisoners' barracks at Tarhuna were now urgently required, so the inmates had to be hurriedly moved elsewhere. The German troops came in, exhausted, with trucks battered. Thus, Stan and the other prisoners knew that something was on the go. They had not seen a single German from Derna up to Tarhunah, almost eight hundred miles.

Suddenly and unexpectedly, they got a shock!

They were herded into trucks, and taken into a transit camp, at Suane Ben Adam, to await shipment to Italy. They were in that camp for ten days, and it remains a nightmare in Stan's memory. Four thousand men were herded into a forest two hundred yards long by one hundred yards wide. All of their blankets were taken away from them. It was a very bitter winter. They were still in khaki summer clothing, and the ground was wet and cold from the rain. To add to this, the camp was lice and flea ridden. If the cold did not prevent one from sleeping, then the hell of resultant irritation from lice and fleas would.

The Italians, jittery as usual, fired shots into the camp if they saw fires burning. All night long, to overcome their fear, they would shout and sing to each other from one sentry's point to another. There were no lights at all

After a while, some prisoners, that were captured on a patrol, came in and said that Allied troops had broken through less than eighty miles away.

Col Di Lana

THE NIGHTMARE MEDITERRANEAN TRIP

The next morning, the prisoners were hurriedly transported to Tripoli Harbour. They set sail as soon as the last man had stepped on board the ship MV *Col di Lana*.

The prisoners were herded, as usual, into the hold, practically on top of each other. Some two thousand prisoners were loaded onto this ship in layers. It was a ten thousand tonner and the first prisoners were placed *down in the bottom of the hold.*

This included Stan Smollan and Harry Khan, who were both members of the Transvaal Scottish. Then planks were laid above them, to accommodate the next layer of prisoners, and so on, until all were loaded. It was an abhorrent situation. To top it all, everyone had dysentery, so if one was on a lower level one was not too well off! Harry and Stan were amongst the first in, and they found themselves near an anchor chain.

Thus began a most horrendous and traumatic trip across the Mediterranean Sea. They went northwards and round Sicily into the Thyrranean Sea to Naples, on the south-west coast of Italy. For the prisoners, the five-day voyage was an absolutely horrendous nightmare.

The Italian sailors were in fear, trepidation and anticipation of being torpedoed. Of course, *they themselves* were dressed in readiness for the plunge, should disaster strike.

Col Di Lana route

The prisoners were not even allowed on deck to exercise. The hold was closed, all but for a plank, three foot wide. Eight latrines were provided for some two and a half thousand men. They were only allowed to go up to the latrines eight men at a time. The ship was unmarked. Thus, the prisoners were in real danger of an attack by the Royal Air Force.

Stan recalled that the only pleasant memory of the voyage was that after a British fighter had attacked the escort, the Italian gunner, seeing another plane coming out of the sun, shot it down with his first burst of fire, only to learn that it was in fact a German fighter.

This performance generated loud roars of approval from prisoners in the ship's holds, and threats from the Italians, to fire on their captives if they did not quieten down. Had that plane attacked and sunk the ship, not many, if any, of the two and a half thousand men would have survived. There were no lifebelts.

It was later discovered, that Allied pilots had orders not to attack merchantmen (non-naval vessels) going away from North Africa, as they might contain prisoners. Previously, one had been sunk off Sidi Rezegh. Somehow, Stan and his co-prisoners had survived the trip to Naples, despite ducking and diving aircraft, submarines etc."

When the *Col Di Lana* put in at Naples, most of the prisoners were in desperately ill health. Nevertheless, they were kept on board for a day. They had not been fed since the previous morning's meal of meat and biscuits. No attempt was made to feed them again until five o'clock the following afternoon. They had endured almost 36 hours without food! Stan was amongst the last to disembark

A few months later, on 18th February 1943 *MV Col di Lana* was to be hit by an aerial torpedo. It was again carrying prisoners of war and it sank

Nightmare memories of this horrendous trip were renewed afresh for Stan, when the current refugee crisis in the Mediterranean began.

CAPTIVITY IN ITALY

After the prisoners were taken off the ship, their situation at long last started to improve. Much to their surprise, they were given a good hot bath and their clothes were steamed to kill the lice. Their spirits lifted slightly, although they were desperately ill, weak, exhausted, depressed and cold.

As newly arrived prisoners on Italian soil, they were assigned to a camp in Capua, a small town not far from Naples (Camp 66). They marched to the camp, and Italian women, for the sight that they presented, buried their faces in their hands and wept. Meanwhile children jeered joyfully!

On arrival at the camp, on 10th December 1942, an amazing sight confronted the captives. Three British sergeants, in new battledress with polished boots, saluted the Italian officer in charge of the prisoners and efficiently obtained orders, as to where the men were to go. How different from the bickering and pleading ways of getting things done that we had become so accustomed to! Here, the Italians were cooperating and prisoners were reciprocating by showing their respect for that cooperation.

Some of the prisoners had vague ideas of an organization called the ***Red Cross***.

Some said that the prisoners actually received British battle dress to wear. Others had heard that the Red Cross operated canteens and sold food to prisoners, in exchange for the one lira per day that the Italian government was to pay POWs.

Some had heard that the men would get one package of concentrated foods per man per month. None of the prisoners, however, after five months of rice and bread, believed that such things existed.

Stan wrote in his journal:

"But what is this! A sergeant says we got a Red Cross parcel with meat, butter, jam, and biscuits. We should get one a week, but there is a shortage for a while, so the issue is half a parcel per week and twenty five "Players" cigarettes. Oh, it's all a bluff. One man comes dashing back wild eyed from a dump with an empty English bully beef tin. 'There are thousands' he yells wildly! We are to discover it is true. Perhaps if those who do the magnificent work of the Red Cross could have seen the men tearing wildly into parcels, their great efforts would have been rewarded.

Receiving these parcels became the one and only thing that kept the men's spirits up. Here was something from home, with English writing on it, to show that we were not the forgotten men, which, during the past five months, we had thought we were.

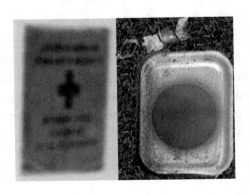

It triggered us to build up our courage. We had received no letters, nor did we expect any for a time yet. The Red Cross parcels gave us the hope and the will to carry on, more so than any other factor I can recall."

In the camp, the order was efficiency and self-respect. Our own internal police were formed to stop the degrading bartering with the Italians. The penalty for an offence was to lose a parcel issue. We got battle dress from the Red Cross and brand new British boots. Now things were in their right perspective. The Italians looked hungrily at our Red Cross parcels. They looked ragged next to our well turned out men. We left that camp over three months after we had landed in Naples. This time the Italian women cheered us for the sight that we presented."

Stan and his comrades were still posted as "Missing, whereabouts unknown". Their families had no idea whether they were dead or alive. They were later classed as "Missing believed Prisoner". This uncertainty went on for almost another year.

Official Red Cross Report on Camp 66, printed in the May 1943 issue of the British Red Cross magazine 'Prisoner of War
PG66 Transit Camp, Capua, Italy

Capua is a very large camp used as a quarantine and transit camp and the strength varies from day to day. At the time of the visit there were 127 officers and 5,000 other ranks. It is situated in flat ground in a mild climate. A new officers' section is almost complete. It will consist of stone bungalows, with washroom, showers dining room and common room. At present the officers are housed in wooden huts.

'Six out of eight sections for other ranks are complete. The remaining two sections are still under canvas, but they should all be in huts by now. Sanitary installations are well constructed and there is an ample supply of water. Electricity is now satisfactory. Each section has its own kitchen and the POWs prepare their own food.

'Three Italian doctors and six Prisoner of War doctors work in the camp infirmary. There is an excellent delousing plant. There are two C of E chaplains and an Italian priest in the camp.

'Kitchen gardens extend between the barracks and also outside the camp. Pigs and rabbits are kept in the camp. A football ground and tennis courts are being made. Some clothing has been distributed by the Detaining Power, but stocks are needed as Prisoners of War arriving at the camp must be fitted out. There is a good stock of Red Cross parcels. (visited November)'

FARA SABINA
P.O.W. CAMP 54

20th March 1942. The prisoners were now on their way to a permanent camp – a camp which had been chosen by the enemy to be their home for the duration of the war. The usual rumours reported good conditions, namely sports fields, wireless, swimming bath etc. The camp was located about 22 miles (35 km) from Rome. Its official designation was Fara Sabina, P.G. 54. As most of the men would have known by then, the letters 'P.G.' stood for *Prigione di Guerra* (Prisoners of War).

The journey was made on third class German trucks. The convoy travelled to a point over eighty miles from Capua, where it turned off, and from there the men were driven another three and a half miles to their destination.

On their arrival on 22nd March, they once again received an appalling shock! To their consternation, they did not see the rumoured sports grounds and canteens, nor any brick barrack-rooms. The stark reality that confronted the weary prisoners was of the tents they were going to live in, surrounded by a sea of mud.

Hoards of wild-eyed, hungry men inhabited the camp. In all, some 4000 lower-ranked prisoners were held there, in two compounds of tents. They were in the main British, South African and Gurkha (Nepalese merchant soldiers) taken at Tobruk.

There existed the old North African spirit of non-cooperation on the part of the Italians. Parcel deliveries were irregular, and there was no battledress. As an inducement, the guards gave men who '*volunteered*' for work two Red Cross parcels and double rations, in addition to a suit of battledress. If the guards wanted a hundred men and only ninety volunteered, they conscripted an additional ten. If there were enough parcels left over, they issued them to the rest in the camp.

The parcels arrived by train from Genoa. Each consignment was enough for a week's issue. Consequently, yet again the prisoners were in constant dread of hunger. Of course, there were, as usual, elements in the camp that disregarded and abandoned their self-respect. They bartered with the Italians, and rummaged through refuse pits for cabbage scraps. These scrambles became so serious, that in order not to endanger the cooks carrying waste to the pits, the wild pack were held back, until the basket was emptied. Then there would follow a mad dogfight for this unspeakable *'food'*.

Stan recalled the different kinds of prisoners who shared their confinement. Some hundreds of French Foreign Legion prisoners arrived at the camp. The French Foreign Legion is a wing of the French Army. It was created in the early nineteenth century, for foreign nationals willing to serve in the French Armed Forces, under the command of French officers.

These Legionnaires were ragged and filthy, but their visibly extreme discipline was magnificent. The Spanish were the predominant race in the Legion. Most of them had escaped into France during the civil war, and had been interned. They were offered the Legion as an alternative to internment. Most of the others were civil prisoners and got into the legion in the same way. Many were outstanding characters, some from fine homes and well educated.

French Foreign Legion

Each of them had some mysterious mishap in their lives, which ended up taking them to the Legion. They would tell the other prisoners of anything except what led them to the Legion. They spoke of terrible hardship and iron discipline. Poor food and irreplaceable bad clothing was the general order. They were taken on long foot patrols into the desert for weeks on end. Their main occupation was the construction of roads, with crowbars and light equipment only. Some went as far as to consider that prisoner of war life which included Red Cross parcels, clothing and boots was the easiest and most pleasant time that they had had since the Legion. Some elements of them not only partook of cabbage scrambles, but also went so far as to stew a cat, which they had caught in the camp, in wine. This they regarded as a delicacy in the Legion.

Stan recalled that much of POW life revolved around plans of escape. Amongst the various underground activities that were in operation in the camp, was an escape committee. One tunnel was detected whilst under construction. Another tunnel, planned partly by Welsh miners, was dug between two barrack rooms, which had just been completed. The tunnel stretched underneath these and under the fence for a hundred yards, till it was to have come out in a thicket. Electric lighting and an air conditioning system were amongst the intricate facilities provided for construction. In all the five months of its construction, the Italians never once detected its entrance, nor did they notice the considerable deposits of earth. On occasions, the committee found it necessary to lead the Italians into believing that a man had escaped, so that

sometime later when he actually did go through the tunnel, he would not be missed. He would have been hiding in the camp itself all the time. In order to create such an impression, the wire needed to be cut.

On seeing this, the Italians would ("in their usual Marx Brothers style") raise the alarm and, after an extensive search, count the personnel of the camp.

In the meantime, a man would hide in the tunnel during the "count" so that it would show up as *one man missing*.

This was so successful, that the committee decided to have some more fun. At the count one morning, four men were hidden in the tunnel. The Italians, gravely concerned, called another count, at which time three were left hidden. The figure was alternated between four and nine during the succeeding counts. The Italians then realised that there was a catch, and thus adopted a new procedure: Round the camp was a six-foot high strand of wire. Two yards away was another six-foot high strand, and two yards from that was a trip wire. This space was "no man's land". Anyone found in there would be suspected of tampering with the wire, and would be shot at. So the Italians decided to check prisoners off by name. They would herd them in between the two six foot strands, and only then look for the escapees inside the camp. This they did most unsuccessfully, so good was the camouflage. In addition and to add insult, for the Italians' effort of herding the prisoners next to no man's land, certain of the chaps joyfully cut the wire, in over a hundred places, whilst the sentries were not looking.

Stan later paid tribute to the Italian officer who, during all these antics, did not impose any reprisals. Rather he said that he respected the prisoners for doing what was their duty as soldiers - to attempt escape.

The prisoners formed a committee for the collection and distribution of news from various sources. There were Italian contraband newspapers, which were strictly illegal in the camp. British pamphlets, which were aimed at the Italians, were smuggled into camp. Radio news (which was not so reliable) was given to the prisoners by a third party Italian.

The newspapers were obtained by bartering Red Cross articles, such as soap, cigarettes and chocolates, which the Italians had not seen for some time. Whilst these papers bore overt German propaganda, the chaps were nevertheless able to build up quite a clear picture of the situation, by following enemy admissions closely, and considering their claims conservatively. In most cases, they guarded their admissions, for example, by asserting that they had inflicted such serious losses on the English, that the taking of such and such a place had not been worth the tremendous loss of men and material.

With the end of the war in North Africa, the invasion of Sicily, the bombing of Rome and the fall of Mussolini, the men in the camp were progressively worked up to a tremendous pitch of excitement in anticipation of events to come. Speculation was in instances so correct, that in many cases prisoners had forecast events to Italian soldiers, and these events actually occurred later on. Wild rumours were circulated amongst the Italians as a result, and these rumours eventually found their way to Rome. At one stage, the Italian commandant gave a pep talk to his men, urging them not to listen to rumours, and especially not to take notice of prisoners of war. Later, because of this kind of speculation, the Italians became convinced that the prisoners had a radio. They sprung daily surprise searches on the camp. During these raids, they took such articles as small knives and scissors, which they thought might be used for escaping. In most cases, these knives and scissors had been bought in their own canteens.

In the meantime, the arrival of Red Cross food and other articles was playing its part in wearing down Italian morale. The same "gentlemen" who so successfully bartered with their captors in North Africa, proceeded to fix various rates of exchange with the sentries, at the usual profit. The articles most required by the Italians were seemingly soap, tea or chocolate. When a sentry beat was changed, it was not unusual to see firstly the ammunition handed over, and then the loaves of bread supplied for bartering.

Eventually the prisoners moved to a new wired compound into barracks. When leaving their old quarters, the prisoners had discarded a number of articles of torn clothing and Italian soap. Italian soldiers were later witnessed in a dogfight for possession of these articles, which had been abandoned by prisoners of war. Stan was told that tea was worth four hundred lire per four ounces at one stage. This was about four pounds sterling. Two ounces of soap fetched about the same. At every opportunity, the chaps had attempted to impress their Red Cross articles on the Italians. When going on an occasional march, in smart battledress and new polished boots, the prisoners proved such a contrast to the Italians' own soldiers, that we were often cheered in the streets.

Stan recalled:

"A most regrettable incident occurred one day in the camp. An Italian soldier coming off duty was walking down the slope towards the guardroom. At the same time he was unloading his rifle, which pointed towards the camp. It accidentally went off. A prisoner who was asleep in bed was killed outright. The Italian major was most upset. He ordered a military funeral with full-honours for the dead man, and bought a tombstone. He told the captors that he realized that this must have now lost the Italians even the very little respect that the prisoners had had for them. The guilty sentry received a very heavy sentence. Thereafter, a concrete box was built, into which the sentries had to load or unload their weapons."

It was in early January 1943, that the lads learned of the Allied invasion of Tunisia, and things began to improve, partly through an improved sign of friendliness by the Italians, and partly through the efforts of men in the camp.

In the camp, the men became very alert and active. Prisoners were, apart from educational activities, passing the time by turning out the most remarkable articles, some of which have been on display in the Transvaal Scottish Museum in Johannesburg.

These articles were constructed, from food tins received from the Red Cross, using primitive handmade tools. Jam tins would be diligently opened up, flattened and joined together. Up to two hundred tins were turned into a perfectly strong suitcase. Pots and pans, which did not leak, were made in the same way, as well as other amazing articles. Some were made from bones, others carved from blocks of wood.

Stan said of these articles: *"At an exhibition, I don't think that a display such as that could have been equalled for its ingenuity or for the diligence of the makers."*

Very few educational books were available. However, men with specialized knowledge of all subjects came forward to conduct classes or to lecture. An excellent debating society was formed. The standard of general knowledge from South African, New Zealand, Canadian, British and American soldiers was exceedingly high. Parcels arrived and spirits were generally high and hopeful through the news. The debating society debated joyfully on: *"When in Rome do as the Romans do"*.

Books began to arrive. Literary critics judged a book by its length, not by its quality!. The prisoners exercised regularly, and interested themselves in various activities. Thus these inmates went about acclimatising to POW life. All in all, they apparently did the best that they could under the circumstances.

Stan told me of life in the camp:
"While some POWs later spoke bitterly of their treatment at the hands of their Italian captors, and the deprivations they had endured, My sentiments are that under the circumstances, the Italians tried their best.

I was one of a number of Jewish prisoners in the camp. I was never ever mistreated because of this. Nor, for that matter, did I ever experience anti-Semitism at the hands of my fellow soldiers.

One cannot over-state the importance of the Red Cross parcels; once these began arriving, the prisoners' situation took a dramatic turn for the better. We suddenly found ourselves 'in the pound seats'. The accepted practice was for each parcel to be shared between two prisoners. The parcels themselves typically contained cigarettes, tea, jam, salmon and all sorts of things. These items then became a sort of currency, through which the prisoners, and their equally needy Italian guards, did a brisk trade.

The tea (and the rest) was very valuable. So the situation would be that one would see an Italian soldier with his rifle on the ground and the prisoners would be throwing a packet of tea over the strands of barbed wire, and the soldier would be throwing over four loaves of bread, which was the rate of exchange. Ten cigarettes were also worth a loaf of bread. A bar of soap also had its value. However, the chaps quickly saw the opportunity to do some unfair trade with the Italians, who did not know that the tea had already been brewed once or twice, dried on the roof and then repacked, to be traded for bread or whatever. These packets were probably destined for the "black market" in Rome. So this kind of thing went on. The food in the camp wasn't great, but we got enough and were busy building ourselves up again. "

The prisoners thus steadily regained their health and strength.

.

INVASION OF ITALY

After the fall of Sicily in July 1943, the first assault on the Italian mainland was expected. Once freedom of speech was restored, following the overthrow of Mussolini that same month, the Italian papers were openly pro-Allied. What they were pressing for was an armistice in terms of which Italian soil would not be used by the Allies for future operations against the Germans,. The fall of Mussolini had been heralded by headlines like "Long Live the Liberation of Italy".

Benito Mussolini

On the 13th of May 1943, 240,000 German and Italian troops – all that remained of the Axis forces in North Africa – surrendered to the British and Americans. Now the road was open to the next major stage of the Allied counter-offensive against Nazi Germany and her allies in occupied Europe – the invasion of Italy. This commenced two months later on the 10th of July with the Anglo-American invasion of Sicily – Operation Husky.

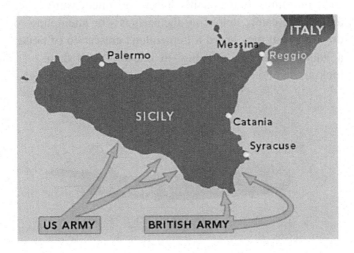

For Benito Mussolini and his Facist regime, the invasion was *the beginning of the end.* The Italian people wanted overwhelmingly, out of a war that had brought them little glory, and a great deal of suffering. Unfortunately, as events were to prove, Germany wanted to protect its forward defensive positions to prevent an occurrence of an outflanking, which would be extremely consequential. At an emergency meeting held on 17th July 1943, Hitler, still personally respectful of Mussolini himself, but by now not troubling to conceal his contempt for the Italian military, effectively told Mussolini, that henceforth, he would be only the nominal leader of an Italy that was in reality under total German military control.

It was at exactly this time that the Allies launched a major air offensive about sixty kilometres to the south of Camp 54 in Fara Sabina.

That morning, Stan and his fellow prisoners were lying around the camp, delousing themselves - or attempting to do so - when they heard a tremendous crescendo of noise, a thunderous roar, growing in intensity and then. . . . looking up into the sky, they saw and heard the bombing!

B-24 Liberator

There was wave after wave of aircraft, an armada of RAF bombers, escorted by fighters, reported later to include over a hundred and fifty B-29 Superfortresses (each with a twenty ton bomb load) and roughly a hundred and fifty B-24 Liberators.

B-29 Superfortress as used later for atomic bomb attacks on
Hiroshima and Nagasaki.

The lads witnessed the aircraft clearly weaving and "sort
of signalling" – the pilots knew that the prisoners were
there. This was a massive show of force. Then the lads
saw the Ack-Ack puffs and heard the sound of bombing.
Debris was rising into the sky. This came from the rail
yards in Rome. Stan later learned that a precision daylight
attack on Rome had taken place. The resultant noise was
unimaginable, and the effect on the prisoners was electric!
Here they were witnessing their own **Allied aircraft on
the attack!** The men ran amuck and the devastated
Italians seemed to run the other way!

Up to now, in the light of the treatment received at certain
camps such as Bengazi, feelings towards the Italians were
emotional. This had reached such depths, that the chaps in
the camp had cheered wildly on seeing hundreds of Allied
planes send up clouds of smoke dust and rubble from the
Rome raid. The hearing in the news of casualties in these
raids had also roused wild cheering. Such was the feeling
and the joy of revenge.

In January 2015 Stan asked me to emphasize:

"Notwithstanding, to this day, I personally have always had the utmost respect for all Italians people"

The Italian authorities were anxious to clear that camp as soon as possible. Thus some were evacuated by ship or submarine, and some were actually reported to arrive in Greece.

The Rome raids, in providing a preview of what lay in store for Italy, should it remain in the war, probably contributed in no small measure to Mussolini's political demise, merely one week later. On the 25th of July 1943 the Fascist Grand Council, at its first and only wartime meeting, voted to dismiss their dictator of 21 years. Henceforth, 'Il Duce' as Mussolini was known, played no more than a marginal role in the unfolding tragedy he had done so much to engineer for his people. Held under virtual house arrest for a time, he was later spirited away in a daring raid by German airborne troops, and he was set up as nominal dictator of the puppet *Salò Republic* in the northern part of the country.

In 1940, Mussolini had taken his country into World War II on the side of Nazi Germany but met with military failure. By 1945, he was reduced to being the leader of a German puppet state in northern Italy and he was faced with the Allied advance from the south and an increasingly violent internal conflict with the partisans. In April 1945, with the Allies breaking through the last German defences in northern Italy and a general uprising of the partisans taking hold in the cities, Mussolini's position became untenable. On the 25 of April he fled from Milan, where he had been based, and tried to escape to the Swiss border.

He and his mistress, Claretta Petacci, were captured on the 27th of April by local anti-fascist partisans near the village of Dongo on Lake Como. Mussolini and Petacci were summarily shot and executed the following afternoon, two days before Adolf Hitler's suicide. Finally, only two weeks before the end of the war, the bodies of Mussolini and Petacci were taken to Milan, and left in a suburban square, the *Piazzale Loreto*, for a large angry crowd to insult and physically abuse. They were then hung upside down from a metal girder above a service station on the square.

Initially, Mussolini was buried in an unmarked grave but, in 1946, his body was dug up and stolen by fascist supporters. Four months later it was recovered by the authorities, who then kept it hidden for the next eleven years. Eventually, in 1957, his remains were allowed to be interred in the Mussolini family crypt in his home town of Predappio.

Source: Wikipedia

Milan, Italy, The hanging of Mussolini and his cohorts.
Belongs to collection: Yad Vashem Photo Archive
From right to left: Starace, Pavolini, Klara Petacci (Mussolini's mistress), Mussolini, Gelormini, Bombacci.
Submitted by: Mordechai Weissman

ARMISTICE

For the next six weeks, Italy was theoretically under the control of a non-Fascist government headed by Marshal Pietro Badaglio. A lame-duck administration, its leaders sought desperately to cut a deal with the Allies through which it was hoped that a prolonged war on Italian soil could be avoided. On the 3rd of September 1943, an armistice was secretly concluded, whereby Italy agreed to surrender unconditionally to the Allies, with the agreement to be announced on 12th September, in order to enable the Italian government to prepare to resist the inevitable German counter-reaction. Neither the Allies nor the Germans trusted the Badaglio administration. The armistice was announced, on 8th September 1943, four days before the date agreed. The Germans on the other hand, were protecting their forward lines of defence, so as not to risk encirclement and thus lose their entire army in Italy.

Even before the armistice was announced, the invasion of the Italian mainland had begun. All this was just the beginning of what would be a prolonged and brutal slogging match. Over the next twenty months American, British and Commonwealth troops, doggedly resisted every step of the way by the German occupying forces, slowly and painfully forced their way northwards up the Italian peninsula until achieving a dearly bought final victory, before the end of the war in Europe.

Not knowing what the future held, prisoners at Camp 54, Fara Sabina reacted euphorically, when the news of the armistice reached them, on the night of the 8th of September 1943. Wild bursts of cheering could be heard. Half the camp was running from the top downward to tell the rest of the men that the war was over, and the other half were running up to find out what had happened.

Later, the camp leader brought the official news. His words were, "I can only tell you that the Italians have asked General Eisenhower for an armistice, which request has only just been granted. We now only have one toast" - and he commenced the strains of "God Save the King" which prisoners had been strictly forbidden to sing during their captivity.

Wild scenes took place. A POW's way of celebrating is to have a 'brew' of tea. This had been denied by a shortage of wood, but now huge fires were made from beds, doors, windows or anything inflammable. The band came out and for that night hardly any of the men stopped to think of what the Germans might do about the armistice, but all got rid of the pent up emotions in a mad orgy of celebration.
The next morning, however, Stan and his fellow prisoners found the camp guarded as strongly as ever. They were warned that anyone attempting to escape would be shot. Orders had been received by the guards that they should protect the captives from the Germans, until the British or Americans had arrived. In the event of German attempts to attack the camp, the gates were to be opened, for the men to scatter. The prisoners were furnished with news, which was unreliable, for it was from the Italian

transmission in London, which already enthusiastic for the benefit of the Italians, had been translated into English by an even more enthusiastic Italian interpreter, who announced: *"The Germans are fleeing right up to the north. They only stop for water, food and cattle, but might take a few prisoners on their way."* In addition to this the Germans, who had seized Rome Radio, were putting out false reports of German landings on all parts of the coast northwards of the camp.

Photo: timesofmalta.com
Italian General Giuseppe Castellano signing, on behalf of Italy, the Italian armistice at Cassibile, Sicily, on September 3, 1943.
Looking on are Italian aide Luigi Marchesi, left, and General Walter Bedell Smith.

On the day the armistice was announced, German forces moved in to seize control of Rome from the Italian Patriot forces. These were regular troops, combined with the Carabinieri, (military police) operating under the authority of the Badaglio government. Despite being heavily outnumbered, the Germans gradually gained the upper hand in the course of three days of stiff fighting, thanks in part to their superior Panzer component, to which the Italians had no effective answer.

ROAD TO ESCAPE

On the 10th of September 1943, Stan and his fellow prisoners had a grandstand view of what seemed like three hundred German paratroopers descending on the Rome airfields. That afternoon, at 4.00 pm, the city surrendered to the Germans. The immediate result of the fall of Rome was that the Italian prison guards lost their courage, got into civilian clothes and fled. The following day, the prisoners awoke to find the camp completely unguarded.

About two thousand prisoners took advantage of their abandonment to break out. Large groups of chaps decided to remain in a group of over a thousand, and make their way, as a body, to the men at Salerno, one hundred and seventy miles away. This obviously proved fatal. The Germans, the same who had paratrooped on Rome, arrived a few hours afterwards and, after finding the camp empty, raked the bush with machine gun fire. To this reception, some five hundred men surrendered. Others kept their hiding places and escaped unnoticed. The other large party found it impossible to find food and water for so many, so they split up into small groups of four to six men. Some proceeded southwards towards their troops, then almost two hundred miles away, and others, finding Italian civilians to be remarkably friendly, stayed where they were, to await release by Allied forces.

The prisoners' celebrations had in fact been premature - liberation was not at hand. Shortly after the mass escape, the camp was once more secured, and most of those prisoners who had left had been recaptured. Stan later learned that the Italian commander of the camp was shot by the Germans. The subsequent story of the P.G. 54 inmates is darkened by tragedy.

There was a reported incident, that on the 28th of January 1944, the camp was completely evacuated and the prisoners – by that stage numbering some 1100 British, South African and Americans – were put on a train to be taken to a camp in Germany, ahead of the Allied advance. While still inside Italy, the train was hit by American bombers, when it crossed a bridge on the Ponte Paglia in Allerona, Italy. There were reportedly over 400 British, U.S. and South African casualties and deaths. They were being transported to Germany in unmarked cattle cars.

The POWs had been padlocked in the cars and were crossing the bridge when B-26s of the 320th Bombardment Group arrived to blow up the bridge. The driver stopped the train on the span, leaving the prisoners, who were locked inside, to their fate.

They came under heavy attack by the American 320th Bombardment Group. The latter, naturally, were unaware that there were Allied prisoners on the train. The bombs hit their targets, destroying ten cars and derailing three others, with the remainder being buckled up in an arch. Many prisoners were either killed outright, or succumbed to their injuries shortly thereafter. Many of them would have been personally known to Stan. He could easily have been one of them had he not escaped.

About a hundred Germans were also killed. According to eyewitnesses, several prisoners were shot by the German guards, who in the chaos suspected them of being part of an escape plan. It was one of the worst "friendly fire" incidents suffered by either side during the entire war. Those who survived the tragedy ultimately wound up in POW camps in Germany, for the remainder of the war, whose end was still more than a year away.

A handful of prisoners - about twenty in all – did manage to evade recapture, after leaving the camp at Fara Sabina. One of them was Stan Smollan, together with Cedric Whitelaw, Ron Tacon, Bill 'Tubby' Trout, Colin Stewart and Basil Hall. These six prisoners realised that the Germans would probably react fast, and that they should be well away when the Germans did arrive. Therefore, it was immediately decided to open the wire and go up into the mountains for a few days until, as it was hoped, Allied troops would arrive to release them. The six of them ran off in a group, haring it to the nearest mountain village. They carried with them enough food for seven days, and warm clothing to carry them through for some time.

Stan recalled:
"After a week, we six fugitives were met by remarkable signs of friendliness, enthusiasm and emotion from the local people. They took us to their villages and gave us food and wine. The women cried, and told us that they prayed and hoped for the day of

liberation by the Anglo Americans. Mussolini and his Fascists were cursed for the way they had swindled them. They spoke of how their golden wedding rings and other jewellery had been taken, to obtain foreign currency during the period when international sanctions were imposed, in response to the Italian conquest of Abyssinia, in 1935.

In place of their gold jewellery, each of them had been given a steel wristband with the inscription, ORO ALLA PATRIA which means *"Gold to the Fatherland"*.

Donation receipt of a wedding ring on the Day of the faith

Images: Wikipedia

Milan, delivery of engagement rings and gold

ITALIAN COMPASSION

"I shall never forget the overwhelming kindness of those who gave me and my companions sanctuary"
Stan Smollan July 2015

Undoubtedly the actions of the Italian rural peasants who defied German warnings of dire consequences (from burning of their homes to execution) demonstrated the extreme courage and compassion of these fine people.

The Six Escapees disguised as Contadini (Italian peasants) [Stan on extreme right]

The *Contadina* (women of the fields) brought hot meals down to the Stan and his fellow escaped prisoners in the fields, and told them to eat as much of their fruit as they could lay their hands on. In many cases, the hot meals were in pots large enough for about twelve men, and were carried for several miles down mountain tracks by women, and balanced on their heads all the way. Some women loaded cooked meals on donkeys and went out in search of prisoners. It became the fashion for a peasant family to be harbouring at least two Allied prisoners of war. Sometimes food arrived as many as six times a day from different people, all of whom expected that the escapees were still starving, and were offended if the escapees did not eat. Food became embarrassingly plentiful instead of a problem. Some villagers tried to outdo the others by offering bigger and better barns to sleep in, more meals a day, and coffee in the morning. Some of them, on arriving with food found others feeding the escapees, and an argument immediately ensued, as to *who had seen the men first and as to whose property the men were.* These arguments entailed much waving of arms and gesticulations, in true Marx Brothers style.

During all these performances, the lads merely had to stand by and watch the fights for possession of them. They had nothing to offer in return, nor would these simple people accept anything whatsoever from them.

The lads were quickly picking up some basic Italian, and the villagers immediately translated the lads' names into the Italian equivalents, so that they could appear more friendly and loving. Sometimes the men went to the villages at night. As the villagers passed by, they would recognise them and one of the men would then feel an arm on his shoulder and a whisper of "good evening English friend. Have you got food and a place to sleep in?" The lads replied "yes" and the villagers would say something like "Thanks to G-d. I have a relation, a prisoner. Perhaps he's looked after too. Be careful. Look out for the Germans. They are beasts. Please G-d the English will be here soon and both you and I will be free again."

The men were fed with bread, macaroni and a concoction of mealie (maize) meal, potatoes and on very rare occasions, a small bit of meat. After all, these contadini had very little themselves.

The bread was flat and in very large loaves. These they cut in half, poured on olive oil and then salted them. Small as the villagers were, and undernourished as they might have been, they had tremendous appetites, and Stan was sure that they ate three times as much of this, an unbalanced diet, as the fugitives would eat of a balanced diet.

Factory-made macaroni had been off the market for a long time. Their macaroni was made from sifted grain. This was mixed with water only, because they had long since been robbed by the Germans of their poultry and eggs. This homemade macaroni was then dipped into hot water and drained off. Then tomato juice, garlic and salt was poured on, to take away the heavy taste. The potatoes were much the same. They were dipped into this "flour" and got the usual bit of tomato and garlic. The mealie meal was the most remarkable. This, after being cooked until thick, was poured onto a large table six by four foot and allowed to set, about a quarter inch thick. The inevitable tomato and garlic were then poured on, and upwards of ten people sat around the table and picked bits off with a fork. It became quite exciting towards the end, when a small amount was left in the centre of the table. This being the most abundant of the food stocks, it was, together with bread and wine, the lads main diet. They called it "yellow peril" because of its colour.

When eating with these simple folk, it was required that on taking the first spoonful one should exclaim "*molto buona*" (very good). Otherwise it was thought that one did not like their food. It was also deemed an insult to the quality of the meal, if one did not make a noise while eating, or belch loudly afterwards.

The mountains to which the lads had fled formed part of the Apennine Chain, the geological backbone of the Italian Peninsula. Stan fondly remembers the simple, self-contained world of Italy's mountain communities of those times. Most of the Italian villages in the Apennines are situated high up, right on the top of mountain peaks, sometimes three to four thousand feet up. The clouds come down low and encircle them, giving the impression of a castle in the clouds, as seen in fairy stories. Because these villages are all on peaks, one could not walk for more than about four miles in the central Apennines without seeing such a village.

They were all thickly populated and the inhabitants lived in the most unbelievably filthy conditions, with a complete disregard for any sanitary arrangements whatsoever. In the valleys below, every available inch of land was cultivated, even onto extremely steep slopes of mountain. It was a miracle of diligence, how they got their oxen to move their primitive ploughs up such slopes. Their ploughs were made from huge tree trunks, and the blades, as well as any other utensils, were made in the villages. Each village had a blacksmith and a boot maker. In fact, they were able to carry on their daily lives without any help or interference from the outside world. One family who had lived twenty miles from Rome all their lives had neither seen the city, nor did they wish to! They worked their land and lived in it.

Grapes were grown, not on vines, but upwards   round apple trees, so that the same ground could be used to grow grain, maize or beans.

In most cases, over eighty per cent of the available ground round a village was owned by one man. He allowed others to use the land for cultivation, the condition being that he got twenty per cent of the total crop. The same thing applied to fruits. Grapes, even after giving up 20 per cent, were firstly hand pressed, to get the best wine. The remnants were sent to the one and only press in the village, and once again, 20 per cent of the wine was taken. The owner of this press then sold his 20 per cent in the village canteen.

Every village had its town crier, and a set of bells, which rang on every quarter hour from dawn to dusk. They rang a specific number of bells if a man died, and a specific number in the case of a woman or a child dying. At dawn, the bells rang to bring the peasants to their work, and minute by minute, the voices grew louder as they poured down the hills, until after half an hour, the place was a buzz of happy voices and hoes clicking against the stones.

The girls picking olives wore picturesque antique styled costumes of pretty colours, and sang during their work. Sometimes, after recognizing the chaps as English, they ran up and gave them bread and fruit, and sang for their English 'brothers'.

THE VENETONNIS

At Montorio Romano, Stan and his comrades were befriended, and taken under the wing of an elderly Italian couple, Berchina and Attilio Venettoni and their family. These kindly people undertook to look after the escapees for two nights. However, at considerable life-threatening risk to themselves, the Venetonnis continued to provide the lads with food and clothing, and in the daytime, hid them in caves in the valley. This was extremely uncomfortable, but they were young and determined to survive. Mostly, Stan and the lads appreciated the courageous and unconditional friendship of this brave family.

Attillio and Berchina Venettoni

The Venetonnis nursed the lads back to good health. They would provide this crucial assistance and take care of the fugitives, for the next three and a half months.

During this period, the six original fugitives from the POW camp were joined by several other escapees, amongst them Royce Schulman and Bill Berridge. Royce had been at school with Stan at Parktown Boys' High, and he was also Jewish. Before his initial capture, he had served as a Lance-Bombardier with the Natal Field Artillery, and had since escaped twice from captivity – once at the time of the original break-out, when the camp guards had abandoned their posts, and again after having been recaptured. Before the war, Bill Berridge had been a junior reporter at the *Rand Daily Mail* in Johannesburg, a job he would return to after being discharged from the army.

The Venettoni family consisted of Attillio and Berchina, their son Piero, and the family mule, who carted bags of building sand from the caves. The house was on a hill. Below that was a barn, where the six escapees slept, on a bed of hay. The caves were lower down, and they only went into them during the day. Life in the valley was like being in a Garden of Eden, with marvellous fruit including apples, grapes and peaches and vegetables of all descriptions. Tasty hot food was brought to the lads by the Venetonnis. Sometimes in the daylight, when they thought the coast was clear, the four would take a chance and bathe in the stream.

Very early on having arrived in this area, the lads made contact with the Italian underground and British agents who, amongst other things, supplied them with civilian clothing.

At night the lads would make their way to the Venetonni family house, in pitch dark. They got to know every pebble and every inch. At the house they listened furtively

to the BBC, which, with its signature tune introduction, the opening bars of the Beethoven Fifth Symphony, *"Da da da da . . . .da da da daaa"* was a ray of hope to all friends of the Allies, affected by the war. This was in fact the voice of hope for Europe. Italians were urged to support the prisoners, and told that they would be rewarded.

GERMANS IN THE AREA

German activity in the area was being stepped up, making the escapees' position, and that of their hosts, increasingly hazardous. During this time, the enthusiasm of harbouring prisoners had worn off, and had been replaced by a considerable fear of German reprisals. The German authorities had knowledge of the prisoners' presence. They had conducted wide searches, using machine guns and grenades. If prisoners were found in a barn, the barn would be burnt down. The owner and his whole family would then be taken off and wouldn't be heard of again. The Germans offered a reward of 1800 lire for every Allied prisoner handed over. This did not affect the defiance of those fine peasants, who continued to feed the men. However, they begged them not to come into the villages, but to keep hiding in the fields. In some cases, they had German soldiers billeted (accommodated) in their villages. The villagers were ordered to cook the Germans' rations. In some instances, German soldiers gave them cigarettes to augment their ration of bread. The peasants regularly brought the cigarettes and some German tinned meat down to the escaped British prisoners.

The lads had, up to then, had few cigarettes, and had even resorted to trying to smoke grape bark or walnut leaves. The grape bark rolled in newspaper, if puffed on too hard, shot out a flame. So they thought it best not to smoke it. Later, the Italians gave them uncured leaves, about two foot-long. These, they cut up with knives and rolled in newspaper, and although very strong to smoke, they found it quite soothing, and were glad to have at least that. Sometimes the villagers even gave the lads part of their own weekly ration of 25 cigarettes, again demonstrating their astonishing generosity.

Some remarkable behaviour by German soldiers also occurred. One of them, spotting the chaps going into a village, recognized them and shouted: "Have you got a coat?" On hearing a negative reply, he said "You will be cold", and drove on.

One crowd of escapees were asked by an Italian fascist to go to the village for food. On arrival, they were betrayed to the German officer, who later released the men since *"it was a dirty trick!"*

Another German soldier was detailed to a prisoner of war cage, to take four prisoners, who had just been recaptured, back to the mountains to fetch their kit. On the way, one slipped away. Later the German soldier met two more fugitives, who he took into custody. He gave them a coin to spin, allowing one to go, as he now had five prisoners and was only required and expected to take four back to the camp.

On many occasions, the chaps met Italian soldiers who had walked from France and other occupied territories, where they were doing occupational duties. After the armistice they had fled, and were either going home or trying to cross the German lines to fight with the Allies.

Escape To Anzio

During the period 3rd September to 30th November 1942 Stan, along with two of his friends, had some remarkable encounters with a man who claimed to be acting for the Italian underground movement "*Partito d' Azione*". He presented them with a note from the Eighth Army. The note stated that he could be trusted and should be obeyed.

In view of the various betrayals, they mistrusted the man, but nevertheless they gave him details of their requirements. The lads requested boots or leather, civilian clothes and detailed maps, so that they could make their way to the British lines. The lads were not optimistic of this stranger's fulfilment. Surprisingly, within five days, over 300 maps, specially photographed or reprinted in sections, had arrived, together with boot leather and civilian clothing. Thereafter, when going to communicate with this brave operative, the lads used to come into the village, climb up a twenty-foot ladder and enter into the room. On one occasion, they exited the back room, via the ladder, whilst a German sergeant major entered via the front door.

One day, Berchina Venettoni came running with hot food, screaming '*Tedesco!*' (Germans) and told the fugitives to immediately go deep into the cave where they made a living, bringing out building sand. The next day she told them that the Germans had fired machine guns into the cave. On hearing about the machine gunning, Stan and Colin Stewart discussed the position, and concluded that it was far too dangerous for the Venetonnis if the lads were to remain. Royce Schulman and Bill Berridge said they would leave with them.

Apart from the fear of recapture, if the lads stayed where they were, there was also the real threat to the safety of the kindly Venetonnis, their hosts and protectors, to consider. Once it became apparent that the Germans were searching the countryside, they decided that they should plan to move on and make a break for the Allied lines. They would make use of one of the maps given to them by the underground.

Stan found generally that the average German soldier was well disposed towards the local Italians, and did not take part in the various atrocities perpetrated against them. These atrocities were apparently carried out by specially trained SS troops. Built upon the Nazi ideology, the SS under Himmler's command was responsible for many crimes against humanity during World War II. On Hitler's behalf, Himmler formed the *Einsatzgruppen* (Task forces) and they built extermination camps. As facilitator and overseer of the concentration camps, Himmler directed the killing of some six million Jews, and several million people from other groups, mostly Polish and Soviet citizens.

After the armistice, the Fascists under the Germans called up groups of young Italians for service as labourers. If the required number did not come forward, various villagers would be surrounded, and all the young and fit carried off for slave labour by SS troops. On leaving villages or towns, evacuated under pressure, all young men would be taken off and put in camps for transit to Germany. In some cases British prisoners, disguised as Italians, would be rounded up as such. In these German camps, where Italians were mixed with Allied prisoners, the Italians received shocking treatment, compared to better treatment and an issue of Red Cross parcels to Allied prisoners.

The maps, which bore the heading "From Italians fighting for freedom, to Allied Prisoners of War", were brought, together with civilian clothes, in a suitcase by a 24-year-old girl. This courageous young woman had travelled by bus from Rome, through German control posts.

The materials given to the escaped prisoners represented a tremendous sacrifice. The Italian peasants themselves had hardly any clothing. Nor could they obtain any boots or have boots repaired. Yet they saw to it that these items reached the lads. Some eighty fugitives were thus equipped. Boots, rarely obtainable on the black market, were sold from £30 upwards per pair. These benefactors were undeterred by the fact that the Germans were looking for escaped prisoners, and of the serious consequences if they were to be caught meeting the fugitives, let alone assisting them.

In light of the dismal display of their military during World War II, jokes about Italians have since often been about their supposed lack of courage in battle.

Stan asked me to emphasize: *"**It is important to remember the incredible heroism displayed by so many ordinary Italian people, during the German occupation.**"*

With the southward flight of the Badaglio government after the fall of Rome, and imposition of German military rule, implemented in part through Fascist Italian surrogates, armed bands of Italian partisans conducted a guerrilla war against the Germans and their Italian collaborators.

In due course, helping escaped prisoners to reach Allied lines, or alternatively to escape to neutral Switzerland to the north, became an important secondary function of these groups. In time, a coordinating body known as the *Committee for National Liberation* was formed, to head up the resistance movement, which was in turn supported by the Allies and the Italian government in exile. The resistance took various forms, including assassinations, hit-and-run surprise attacks and various acts of sabotage. These were frequently met by the Germans with brutal counter-terror operations, including summary executions and mass reprisals against civilians.

On a number of occasions, entire villages were all but wiped out in revenge for German soldiers killed, *regardless of whether the inhabitants had been involved or not!* An estimated 15,000 Italian civilians were murdered in this way during the German occupation. This illustrates the kind of risks that people like the Venetonnis were taking in giving sanctuary to escaped Allied prisoners. It should also be a reminder of the sheer evil of the Nazi regime, that many brave young men had joined up to fight against, notwithstanding that the previously recorded instances of decency, that they experienced at the hands of individual German soldiers, should likewise not be forgotten.

Taking part in actual military operations was only one way of serving in the underground. There was also a range of vital supporting services that needed to be provided, such as arms smuggling, the establishment of safe-houses for hiding operatives in transit and for taking care of their wounded, the provision of food and other basic supplies and reliable communications networks.

It was primarily through this clandestine infrastructure that Stan and his companions had been able to remain at large for so long, and which they now would have to rely upon, if their pending bid for freedom was to be successful.

CHALLENGE:

JOIN UP WITH ALLIES

On New Year's Day 1944, Stan and his three companions – the afore-mentioned Royce Schulman, Bill Berridge and Colin Stewart came to a decision to try to make their way through the German lines, and make contact with the Allies. It was something they had been considering doing for a month already. They had frequently been able to tune in to the BBC broadcasts from London. According to the latest news from this source, coupled with information gathered from Berridge and Schulman, who had recently escaped for a second time, from a German camp, it seemed that the lines would be relatively immobile during the winter months up until May, some five months hence. This was because on such a front, there are many natural barriers of mountains, which are so impassable with equipment, that only their flanks are guarded.

During the previous three months, the Allied forces had been working their way northwards, but it had been slow going. Ultimately, the advance had ground to a halt in the Cassino area, scene of some of the most bitter fighting of the entire war. It was in part as a way of breaking this deadlock, that the Allies would shortly afterwards launch Operation Shingle, through which a new beachhead would be established to the south of Rome, but some way in, to the rear of the German lines.

The main landing point was to be the small coastal town of *Anzio*, an ancient port roughly forty miles from Rome. All this, Stan and his three companions would learn in due course.

Before dawn on 10th January 1944 (which happened to be Stan's 24th birthday) the intrepid four set out. Of course, it was still winter and snow had just started falling. In biting cold and trudging knee-deep through the heavy snow, they made their way down to lower ground. They each carried only the suit of civilian clothes that they stood in, a greatcoat (heavy overcoat) and **enough bread for one meal!**

The four of them did not advance as a group, but in pairs, dodging off the road whenever danger threatened. They made their way to a point as near as possible to the German lines, where the Italians would still feed and shelter them. Nearer to the lines, the Italians wouldn't even talk to an escaped British or Allied prisoner, as they (the Italians) were petrified of being shot by the Germans, as retribution.

Furthermore, the four had no idea if and where they were going to get their next meal. Nor did they know whether they would get shelter that night, or the next night for that matter. However, they obviously had a peculiar confidence, as not only did they always get food, but on only two occasions did they not have shelter.

They had no money, but still they were provided with food and lodging, as they went their way. All they could do in return was to issue what Stan described as *"our own form of credit card"*, written on the back of one of the leaflets dropped by the Allies. These leaflets urged Italians to look after the prisoners of war and promised a reward. The leaflets also asked Field-Marshall Montgomery to recompense each family for their help to the fugitives!

After the war, Field Marshal Harold Alexander, Supreme Allied Commander of the Mediterranean Forces, issued certificates to those who had risked their lives by assisting escaped prisoners of war.

Field Marshal Harold Alexander at his headquarters in the Palace of Caserta, Italy

It was snowing in the mountains, so the four lads set off to the plains, making for Tivoli, just to the north-east of

Rome. In due course, they arrived at the village of Gerano in the Tivoli area. It was warmer there, and they stayed for several days.

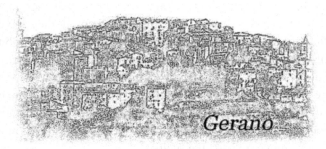

Gerano

They became very involved with the villagers. Up to then the four had not had many encounters with German soldiers. From their hiding places, they had watched the Germans searching for them. Dressed in civilian clothes, the lads had walked past Germans in villages at night, and they had watched long lines of German transport passing along the main roads southwards. In hiding in the fields, they chose villages, which were off main arteries to the south, so that they were able to walk about a little bit and sun themselves. Their chief danger up to then was posed by the Fascist Italians, who would walk around and even talk to escapees as friends, and then betray them to the Germans for the 1800 lire reward. If the four fugitives saw a German they got out of the way, but with Italians they had to rely on their own judgment, and to trust luck. Most times they had no choice but to speak to Italians to get food and information. The average peasant Italian was terribly afraid, and most unreliable for news. In most villages where they had been caught harbouring prisoners of war, such panic had reigned after German reprisals, that they would have no further dealings with prisoners of war, and many prisoners would have to trek elsewhere in search of food. All that Stan and the lads had at stake was their freedom, whereas the Italians risked their homes and even their lives. The Germans often dressed in civilian clothes, and went about telling the Italians that they met that they were British, thus trapping them if they gave them food. The Italians *always* gave the lads at least a bit of bread, and begged them not to stay, pleading of "many spies" and of "hundreds" of Germans in the area. These generally turned out to be a few convalescent German soldiers. Stan found the Italian women to be far more reliable and ready to help them. At the very least, the women never refused the fugitives food.

Stan wrote:

"Our most frightening enemy so far was the weather, now that the winter had set in, and there was heavy snowfall. We each had a suit of civilian clothing. Up to then, each of us had a greatcoat as well. We decided that greatcoats would not be carried any more, as these would immediately arouse suspicion. Thus we abandoned our greatcoats.

Between the four of us, we decided on a most hazardous strategy. Our boots would not be able to last walking the mountains, so instead we walked along the roads, irrespective of whether German convoys passed us! I shall never forget the feeling, when eight German trucks passed us on the road. We looked at them and they looked at us. Just the slightest suspicion and we were on our way to Germany. Remarkably, we had surmounted another obstacle. Frequently practising this audacious behaviour, we passed within a few yards of German soldiers, and sometimes greeted them in Italian. On one occasion we slept in a barn less than 100 yards from a hall in which Germans were billeted."

THE DELELLIS FAMILY

Thus the four men arrived at a location, which they decided upon as a rendezvous point, for the following four months, before they actually attempted to cross the German lines. With the invaluable maps, they knew their exact position, and the distance they needed to go. Thus, they began to seek someone who would be prepared to feed and shelter them for the anticipated four month period.

They met an Italian woman, a middle aged spinster, who was a member of the De Lellis family. On seeing them, Tina De Lellis not only insisted on the lads staying, but she also would not hear of them leaving until the Allied troops arrived. She cried bitterly that the lads would die of cold and hunger. She could never allow that.

Tina herself was an aristocrat, the daughter of a count. Her one brother had died thirty years earlier, and she had been in mourning ever since. She lived with her other brother, in a large house in the mountains. His wife had deserted him 25 years before, and being a devout Catholic, he had never again married.

Tina was emphatic that she was not concerned if the lads were caught there - "They can only shoot me", she said. Their other brother, Tommaso de Lellis, was an officer in the Italian army. By pure coincidence, Tommaso was at that time *a prisoner of war in South Africa!* Stan remembers wondering if Tommaso was being held in the

Zonderwater POW camp, where Stan had himself completed his military training. Over eighty thousand Italian POWs were at one time or another held at Zonderwater during the war.

Tina De Lellis and her brother gave Stan and his companions much more than bare shelter. For about two weeks, they stayed in very decent accommodation, provided by their hosts. It consisted of a completely furnished three-roomed house with a kitchen, near the De Lellis's own home. They were to regard themselves as guests. A servant even waited on them and washed their clothes. They ate at a table with a spotless tablecloth and serviettes, *as a family*. At every meal, the brother would raise his glass and wish them "health and a good appetite". Later they would all sit around the fire and converse, as far as their vocabulary would stretch.

Stan wrote:

"The De Lellis family gave us Italian names, tried to make good Catholics of us, and all in all, treated us wonderfully well. They were good, kind people who unquestionably risked their lives for four young men.

On one occasion, my companions and I went to a nearby village to listen to the BBC broadcast from London. We were wildly entertained in the village pub, for the villagers had seen a few of the British "liberators" for whom they were waiting longingly. On returning to the house, our hosts were both in a state of frenzy and scolded us, in motherly fashion, for staying out late and getting drunk: "You must not do it again."

They had thought the four of us, whom they had so taken to their hearts, had left them. Furthermore, they had heard that we had met some Italian youths playing soccer, and had accepted the challenge of "Italy vs. Sud Africa". Our hosts were rather horrified at us having taken such a chance."

Then, the date would have been the 22nd of January or shortly thereafter. News was received that the Allies had made a landing south of Rome. The Germans had expected a landing to the north of Rome, and the pandemonium that followed helped the four fugitives that were on the run. The Italian underground movement was quite active in the area.

One day, in Gerano, Stan felt a brush on his arm, and a package was put into his hands. This was obviously from a British agent, who immediately disappeared. It was the first time that Stan had seen anything that even resembled money, in a long time. British agents now summoned them, and alerted them to a BBC announcement, that the night before the Allies had landed at Anzio some seventy miles away. The underground gave the escaped POWs maps, illustrating where the landing had taken place.

The maps showed Allied positions at Cassino to the south, where the Germans had established a strong position in and around an ancient monastery. Further down the coast, the Allies had already landed at Salerno near Naples, and now, with the Anzio landings, had invaded at the northern-most point to date. It was evident that there was going to be a battle to the death.

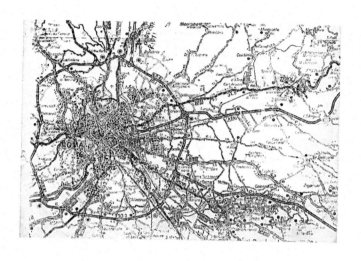

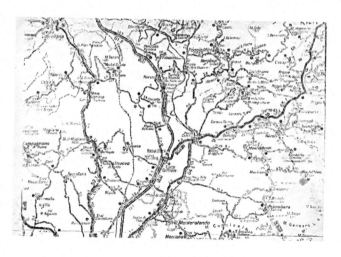

TO ALL ESCAPED ALLIED P. O. W.

1 - The bearer is trustworthy and comes to you in accordance with
    8th army orders.
2 - He will give you instructions for your return into British
    occupied territory.
3 - Pass on the instructions and the maps to all other P.O.W. you
    may know or meet.
4 - Tell no one but POW of the instructions that there are has given
    you and do not show the map to civilians. Destroy it if you
    are captured. Beware of spies.
5 - When travelling keep away from even the smallest roads do not stop
    anywhere more than is strictly necessary. Do not travl tra-
    vel in groups of more than two or three men. Near the lines you may
    find German patrols even in isolated farmhouses and on sheep tracks.
    Therefore be cautious.
6 - Take if possible at least 6 days' food rations and go cross
    country.
7 - The scale of the map is 1:300000 which means that one inch stands
    for 7 miles and 1400 yards on the ground.
8 - Give the bearer receipt for the map with your name, rank
    and number.
            BEST LUCK!

ANZIO

As a military operation, the Anzio campaign was controversial at the time, and remains so to this day. The actual landing on 22nd January 1944 was achieved with remarkably little loss of life. Indeed, caught on the wrong foot, the Germans were unable to mount more than a token resistance.

Nevertheless, no attempt was made, by the Allied commander, Major-General John P Lucas, to press this advantage, for example by moving quickly inland and threatening the German lines from the rear, or perhaps by even making a dash for Rome itself. Instead, the next six days were spent methodically unloading men and materials.

A beachhead no more than two to three miles deep was established before the German counter-attack was underway.

For their part, those entrusted with actually carrying out the operation, insisted that the beachhead needed to be properly secured before any further thrusts inland could be risked. Whichever view one adopts on the question, the facts are, that by the time the Allies were ready to go on the offensive, nearly one hundred thousand Germans, under the overall command of Colonel General Eberhard von Mackensen, had been brought up to resist them. By the end of January, a full-scale battle – aerial, naval and on the ground was underway. In those early stages, the Allies were hard-put merely to hold onto the beachhead, and prevent their enemies from hurling them back into the sea. It was into this hornets' nest that Stan and his companions would shortly be venturing.

When they heard of the Anzio landing, the chaps broke the news to the De Lellis's, of their intention to make a dash for the Allied lines. They both cried bitterly, but stated that if that was what the chaps wanted to do, they should go. They gave the chaps the only and complete ration of meat they had had in weeks. Each of the four was given a written message of *Godspeed*, on a printed visiting card, which they were instructed not to throw away. Tina didn't care if the Germans got it. That is how Stan remembers their parting from the De Lellis family, to whom they owed so much gratitude. Stan's card from Tina has been preserved to this day.

Escape To Anzio

The Allied landings were at two points – at Anzio, and close by, at Nettuno. The underground advised the four Springbok lads to get moving, and see if they could make their way through, to join up with the Allies.

The lads realized that in such a surprise landing, there would be confusion for at least a week. There would be many civilians caught in the battle, unlike the other front, where anyone not in uniform in between the lines was shot at. The four fugitives had lost only forty-eight hours, and walking the roads at a hard pace, they felt confident of being able to cover the 70 miles (112km) in less than four days.

They marched fourteen hours per day, stopping to rest for only one hour on each day.

They refrained from walking at night, because of the danger of advancing headlong into German outposts. At least in the day they had a clear view of what was ahead, and if they ventured upon Germans, the lads could bluff them that they were Italian shepherds looking for lost sheep. As luck would have it for the lads, very few Germans were able to speak Italian.

Allied troops land at Anzio, January 1944

Tanks of an Armored regiment
disembarking from an LST in Anzio

On their third morning out, the four lads heard the guns
and even small arms fire, and saw strafing by the first
American planes that they had seen since Fara Sabina. On
the map, the battle appeared to be developing round a
place called Velletri, which was on the main road south.
Accordingly, they decided to look for a spot which was
less likely to be contested. Long convoys of German
transport tanks and guns could be seen moving in all
directions.

The previous day, they had on occasion seen a convoy
planting an arrow at a crossroads, denoting the direction
in which it had gone, so that the following convoy would
know which way to go.

What posed something of a dilemma for the lads was whether they should just turn the arrow in another direction, or throw it away altogether. The Germans were exceptionally methodical. They were trying to throw an iron ring around Anzio. It made sense for the four to follow the German troops, because where they were going was where the lads themselves wanted to go.

The four of them made their way south-westwards towards the coast, judging by the sound of the guns, and the strategic possibilities on the map. By now they were out of the mountains and approaching the Cisterna di Roma and Pontine Marshes, around which the battle was quickly developing. Cisterna was also guarding the main highway. The Pontine Marshes of Anzio were being drained in fast flowing water to the sea. There was a seven mile-long canal, approximately four foot deep, icy and swift flowing, with six to eight-foot banks, running east to west to the sea. These were called the *Mussolini Canals*. The area is today the site of the Fumicino Leonardo Da Vinci International Airport.

Fumicino Leonardo Da Vinci International Airport

The lads' exhaustion was mounting. The unfolding battle was causing chaos all around them. It was late. They were only managing to move forward on the weight of their bodies. They could hardly bend their legs. Thus they resolved to stop for the night, their third night out.

The problem was to get food, and most importantly shelter, considering their physical state. They had noticed frequently, that Italians were extremely impressed by rank, even if it were only a corporal. The Italians surmised that, particularly near the lines, if they handed any soldiers over to the Allies, particularly officers, they would be well rewarded.

The four lads advanced further into open ground towards the Canal and witnessed horrific destruction . . . They saw injured animals and frantic people, who were by then being bombarded by the Royal Navy. They came across a group of men and women, and told them that they were American paratrooper officers. The group approached them, accepting their verbal identification. The response was incredible. They threw their arms around the four lads. The women, thinking that they had been liberated, let forth screams of *Nostre Salvatori* (Our Saviours), and kissed the lads wildly. One of the men gave Stan a real Russian kiss. *"He rushed at me. I don't know what would have happened if I had sidestepped. There was a 10-foot deep donga [ditch] behind me."*

They took the lads up to a double storeyed barn, in which twenty men woman and children, refugees from Cisterna, were huddled around a fire. As a result of the Allied landing, they had lost everything, but they were overjoyed to be free of the German "beasts". They gave the lads food and wine. They cried and cursed the Germans. Finally, the man and his wife gave the lads their own bed, so that they might rest well. The couple slept on the floor round the fire.

Stan later wrote in his journal:

"Never have I seen such weary, nerve strained and fear bred faces. We lay in bed and listened to German machine gun fire. In the morning, we might be free. I remember looking at the map. Our troops were twelve miles away. The green grain fields were just the same there as where we are. There we are free – here is hell, hunger, cold and fear of capture. It is raining heavily and this saves us from capture by some Germans, who are sheltering in a camouflaged gun pit. We decide to make for the sea, in between our troops' two points of landing, hoping to meet friendly patrols.

As we reached level ground, from where the sea was now visible in the far distance, Royce Schulman, as a trained gunner, was able to estimate that if the four of us were able to get into the canal, the firing would be over our heads."

By some miracle, on day four at around dusk, after walking the massive distance from Gerano, we managed to get into a canal in the middle of the two landings. There was shelling going on overhead, and the Royal Navy was firing in from the sea.

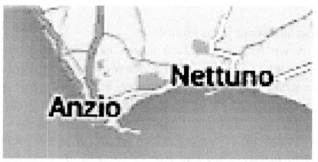

We were now at the Mussolini Canals. The purpose of these was to drain off the Pontine Marshes, which is an area reclaimed from the sea. It was soggy country, on which the grain then flourished, and it was as flat as a pancake. The canal had twenty-foot high banks, in the bed of which ran the water, about four and a half foot deep, with the path on either side. It provided excellent cover, and ran right down before emptying into the Tyrrhenian Sea, near Anzio. By making our way along it, we were able to slip past the main German positions, and this was undoubtedly the saving factor.

As we expected, shepherds were grazing their sheep peacefully, with just the occasional shell falling in the vicinity. Providentially, one of the shepherds warned us of three Germans patrolling the canal, whereupon we decided to make a detour. The country was flat, so we walked in twos, about six hundred yards apart. At one stage, the patrol was in between the pairs. From time to time, we walked past the bodies of dead German soldiers.

We were now coming within sight of the barrage balloons over the beachhead at Anzio. These were low-level type balloons, designed to counter strafing attacks. The balloons could be raised or lowered to the desired altitude by a winch. Their purpose was ingenious: to deny low-level airspace to enemy aircraft. Thereby, the enemy were forced to higher altitudes, thereby decreasing surprise and bombing accuracy. It enhanced ground-based air defenses and the ability of fighters to acquire targets, since intruding aircraft were limited in altitude and direction; and the sight of the cable presented a definite mental and material hazard to pilots.

We had seen soldiers, but thinking them to be Germans, we had given them a wide berth. Later, we learned that they had in fact been American troops. Now we could only move by calculating the direction of the guns and the distance they were firing, by the flash, the smoke and the blast. We realized that we had infiltrated into no man's land, as shells were passing over our heads from either side. Occasionally, some fell a hundred yards away, and we sometimes came upon freshly-made craters, still smoking. It was obvious, by the dead bodies and equipment lying about, that there had been a battle over this ground. The civilians were in a shocking state of fear. Their houses had been hit by shells, and some had been wounded. They were not only afraid to talk to the four of us, but they had been in their cellars under cover for the past three days. People in the crowd were asked if they knew where the Americans were, but they said they had seen neither Americans nor Germans. They did not believe that these four young men were British."

The long adventure was now about to reach its climax. Dramatic concluding moments, when everything that Stan and his companions had struggled for was in the balance:

The fugitives suddenly saw the sea. They saw the German planes meeting a wall of fire from ack-ack (anti-aircraft fire), which had to be Allied. It was dark. They could hardly walk any more, but they decided it was now or never. They made for the canal again, waded across it, and came up the other side, into icy cold water, because they were by now close to the coast. Bitterly cold and dejected, they suddenly heard the words *"Halt. Mickey"* rapped out by a helmeted figure with a rifle. Immediately it passed through Stan's mind that this was the accent of a German!

Stan remembered Colin Stewart saying:
"We're done for - so far and so near!"

They had believed that their line was still a night's walk ahead. "Halt. Mickey" might well be German, but an American speaks in a high-pitched voice like a German. Their helmets are also alike. So, if he is an American, the lads must do the obvious, and shout the second half of the password, which must be "Mouse", and do it quickly. Otherwise they will shoot. They fear answering, in case he is a German, in which case they would have to "spin" the shepherd and the sheep yarn, and trust to luck. On hearing the challenge, two of the lads had dropped to a kneeling position, and they were immediately confronted by a row of steel helmets and rifles, with safety-catches clicking forward. Remember, that the four fugitives were in civilian clothes, they had discarded their maps and they had no identity documents. All this made them liable to be shot on sight.

Fortunately, the NCO shouted out in Italian "come here", before giving a fire order. One of the chaps went over, and on seeing U.S. Badges, and hearing the voice of an American say, *"What the blazes do you guys want here?"*, flung his arms round the American chap, yelling wildly *"We are on your side"*, for which he had a Tommy gun stuck into him, and was told to keep his distance. On hearing that they were Americans, Stan had in his excitement run straight into barbed wire, trying to get across and embrace one of them. The Americans were partly and almost convinced that the four were British, and with a complete disregard, they all lit up cigarettes and had a party right there on the front line. These jollifications were stopped abruptly by an officer, Lieutenant Don Steele, commander of the platoon in that area.

The four were taken to the American headquarters in a farmhouse. Lieutenant Steele told them how lucky they were, as they had entered a high security area.

They were placed under arrest!

He then took the lads and put them up in their sergeants' mess. The four escapees were all in a state of complete exhaustion and really did not know what was going on. They were given hot food and drink, as well as what the Americans called 'K Rations', which was dehydrated food, developed to sustain a soldier for one day.

Stan stated:

"At this point I must pay tribute to my three companions Royce Schulman, Bill Berridge and Colin Stewart. We stuck together through thick and thin. A special tribute is due to Royce Schulman, whose expertise in reading artillery fire had played a crucial role in our escape. It was thanks to his steadiness that we had got through the German lines, taken cover in the Mussolini Canal between Nettuno and Anzio, and finally made it to freedom."

The next day, in the late afternoon, Lt Don Steele reported that he had discussed the lads with his commander, who had said that they should be sent, under escort, to British Headquarters in the region. There was still a great deal of firing going on, as it was only day-five of the landing.

The Americans showered the lads with food and cigarettes. They were given a tumbler full of neat whisky, which Stan said he did not even feel go down, and a sleeping draught. The Americans told them that the last chap who had taken one of the "blue heaven" pills, had slept for 18 hours solid.

They were too overtired to sleep. They sat up and spoke till three in the morning.

Stan reflected:

"I doubt whether in that physical state, and soaking wet in that cold, we could have survived another night in the open!"

In the morning, the Americans asked them how they had got through the minefields. Aghast, the lads answered that they didn't even know that they had walked through minefields. The Americans also related that the night before they had shot one of their own men, for not answering the password correctly, or promptly. This was the lads' first encounter with Americans. On hearing their drawl, for the first time, it made the whole situation appear more sinister and unreal.

Stan wrote:

"It is hard to describe how we felt, because the reality of our freedom had not sunk in, nor did it, until several days afterwards. Even then, it seemed weird to sit down to a meal and eat until we were no longer hungry, or for that matter to eat when we were hungry, or to throw away a cigarette butt."

As South Africans, the chaps found a lot in common with the average American, more so than with the British. Man for man, they too tended to have a higher standard of education. Their discipline was based on a finer understanding between officers and men, who showed respect for one another. In this, a paratroop battalion, officers and men were drawing food in the same queue.

Later, the lads were taken to battalion headquarters with a major. At battalion headquarters, they were, surprisingly, not challenged by the sentry, although they were still less than 150 yards from the front line. All that the major retorted was, "You'd think we paid these guys to keep sentry". All the time, despite their hard fighting of the last few days, and what lay ahead, the American soldiers were more interested in the four South African escapees, who they regarded as veterans. After all, the lads had fought for a year and had been prisoners for a year and a half. For their part, most of the American soldiers at Anzio had been in the army for less than twelve months.

The Americans concentrated on giving the frontline troops the best of rations and equipment. The quality and the ingenuity of their rations was incredible.

The following day the escapees were given a very long interrogation during which they were able to relate much valuable information about gun positions, of which the lads had made a mental note, and of fascist activity at various points along their routes. Their maps had proved to be invaluable.

During the day, the beachhead had been attacked fiercely by German aircraft, and now that the lads were in it, it seemed as dangerous to get out of it. To quote an American "I wouldn't go near that harbour if I was going right to the States. If I were you guys, I'd dig a hole, and stay in it for a few days".

During that afternoon's air raids, whenever an alarm sounded, everyone raced to find cover. A minute afterwards a shout would go out, *"plane coming down in flames"*, and all the Americans would rush out with cameras to film it, apparently quite oblivious of the danger that still existed.

The lads were astounded and open mouthed at all the super equipment, transport and specialist landing craft and tanks that they saw. In their own time, fighting in the desert, they had fought with inferior and obsolete equipment, and even that was short at the time. They had been captured when the Allies were losing the war. Now that they were winning it, *the four lads were free.*

Later the next day at British Headquarters, they came across a gentleman with a band "War Correspondent". He was the well-known, and now famous, Wynford Vaughan-Thomas, editor of BBC Radio News Reel. Vaughan-Thomas chatted to, the lads, and questioned them about Johannesburg, which he was familiar with. He congratulated the lads on their disguise, commenting that they looked more like Italians than any Italians he had seen. It was Vaughan-Thomas who persuaded the British that Stan and his three comrades were **genuine!** He vouched for them, and the next morning they were escorted into the beachhead.

There, a full-scale battle was in progress, involving navy, air force and ground troops.

The lads witnessed countless soldiers with 'unbelievable' equipment, vehicles and tanks, the likes of which they had never seen or heard of before.

At that stage, the Allies were hard-pressed and hanging on for all they were worth.

Men of the U.S. 3rd Infantry Division landing in
late January 1944 (Wikipedia)

Wynford Vaughan-Thomas next took the four to the senior American officer, who was called the "Beach Master", with instructions to put them on an American warship - an LST (landing ship tank).

The four were still under arrest!

It was a Wednesday, and Vaughan-Thomas wanted to put the four newly liberated Springboks, on his BBC show that Friday. He had passed the lads a number of times, while looking for them to make a recording for the BBC News Africa Service. He implored them to stay an extra day, to make this possible. However, the lads were understandably keener, by that stage, on getting onto a ship, and getting to safety at Naples. Thanks to Wynford Vaughan-Thomas's influence and kind efforts, the four men avoided much formality, and were able to embark that same night.

Before doing so, they were interviewed by the Beach Master, Lieutenant Commander John Blakeley Russell, who was not only a high ranking and distinguished American naval officer, but also the director of the whole show. On the beaches, he had before him a complete plan of the disposition of all troops that had disembarked, and of others disembarking by the minute. He would direct them where to go. He was in charge of all comings and goings. Stan likened him to a kind of "specialist traffic officer" for all the troop movements, in and out. Despite this terrific mental strain, Lt. Com. Russell still found time to talk to the four wary lads of their experiences, and to get them onto a boat.

The incoming troops were embarked and ready on their trucks, at Naples in LSTs, which were of about 1200 tons displacement, flat bottomed and on coming up to the beaches, the front had opened up and they drove straight out in convoy, into action wherever required. They carried upwards of 50 tanks or trucks each. Above the tanks were luxury cabins, radios etc., and messes, so that the men might partake of the best. The crews were able to go on under these conditions, from one point to the other . . . indefinitely. They unloaded and reloaded at either end, immediately upon landing. So they put the four lads onto one of these LSTs, bound back to Naples. They were most fortunate and their LST reached Naples unmolested, after 36 hours. They had missed a massive attack on the Harbour by under an hour. A hospital ship had been sunk after 30 raids in two days.

Stan said:

"We had endured yet another mini escape."

HOMEWARD BOUND

On arrival at Naples, the commander wired through to the Port Master that he had four escaped prisoners on board. The port authorities immediately assumed that the prisoners were Germans, and the four lads found American guards waiting to take them to a German prisoner of war cage. The lads were still in civilian clothing, and had been issued with a permit from a British officer to travel in this condition. They were "almost" able to convince the Americans that they were South African. They nevertheless had to go to the prisoner of war cage to await identification. On the way, Italian civilians, seeing the lads under guard, assumed that we were Germans, and tried to attack them with stones. The American troops escorting them, hurried the four out of a nasty situation. Here they were, finally on their own side of the lines, and yet they found themselves locked up again, and attacked by angry Italians!

This was the second time in 13 months that Stan and his comrades had entered Naples. Once, as prisoners they had been starving, and were jeered at by the local populace. Now the lads were free, and the Italians were begging British and American soldiers for food.

An escort arrived and for want of putting the four new arrivals somewhere, until they were identified, the escort put them into an UNRWA (United Nations Relief and Works Agency) camp.

This camp was full to the brim with people of all colours, races and creeds. All were desperate to find some form of sanctuary. The camp contained refugees fleeing into liberated Italy from all corners of Europe - Jews, Gypsies and Eastern Europeans. They all spoke to each other in Italian. The quartet wandered around the camp, witnessing myriad scenes of despair.

In the prisoner of war cage, they found that the suspicion about their identity had been well justified. In the cage, they came across thousands of refugees of a myriad of nationalities. There were, inter alia, Yugoslavs, Poles, French, Dutch, Chinese, Russians, Arabs and Jews from all over Europe, all of whom had escaped from concentration camps, and had been trailing across Europe, running from the Germans. Now the Italian front, the only Allied foothold in Western Europe, was an international exchanging point to freedom. These people, some of them young women and children, crossed the German lines. Amongst them, however, were German spies, posing as these refugees. Other refugees posed as U.S. citizens, hoping to get to America. Thus the four lads, along with all these refugees, had no choice but to await identification. The Americans fed and clad the displaced people until their identity was established.

The lads spent two days there, and had many extremely interesting conversations. All the various nationalities, even the Chinese, spoke to them in Italian. It was the one language, which almost all seemed to be able to make themselves understood in.

Providentially, they then met a South African Jewish army chaplain. He was none other than Reverend Moshe Natas, later to become renowned throughout the South African Jewish community, and beyond, as a devoted Judaic scholar, educationalist and Zionist activist, until he died at the age of 102.

Reverend Natas summoned transport, and the four were taken up to General Poole's Sixth South African Division, at the top of a hill in Naples (in a mansion which incidentally had been the home of Admiral Nelson's mistress, Lady Emma Hamilton). It was very near to, and in sight of Mount Etna. On arrival, still in civilian clothes, they had (what was to them) a historic meeting with a South African officer, whom they greeted with "Bon Giorno, we are South Africans".

Their clothes were burned, and they were deloused. Next, they were given a mass of injections, and put into South African uniforms, for the winter weather.

Stan wrote:

"Thus, we prepared for our homeward trip. It would take some time before we could begin our return journey, and even then, it would take many thousands of kilometers of travelling before we saw South Africa again.

Throughout the five months with the partisans, and on our travels, we never had any money. Within 30 days we were sent by train to the great Italian Naval Base of Taranto, in the boot of Italy.

There the entire Italian Naval Fleet lay in Allied hands. We boarded the Polish converted warship "M.S. Batory" and were transported to Alexandria in Egypt. From Alexandria we travelled by train to Cairo.

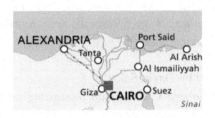

At this stage our families were informed about us, Due to circumstances, we had been listed as 'Missing, believed Prisoner', since the middle of 1942, following the fall of Tobruk. On the 18th of February 1944, in Johannesburg, Mrs Cissie Smollan, my mother,

received an official telegram reading simply: "Department of Defence has pleasure in informing you that your son 27498 Pte Stanley Solomon Smollan arrived Egypt 13 Feb". It was the first news that my mother had received about me in twenty months.

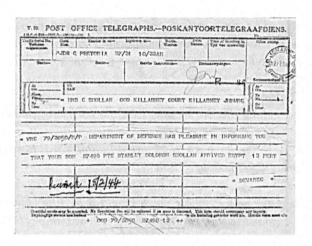

On learning of my escape, my cousin Albert Weinberg obtained leave from his unit to visit me in Cairo. Albert's father, John (Jeannot), was married to my maternal aunt, Dinah."

As reported by David Saks:
"John Weinberg's story is an interesting one, in some ways foreshadowing Stan's own. He and his family came out to South Africa from Kurland, Latvia, in the early 1890s, while he was still a teenager, and settled in Bloemfontein, capital of the independent Boer Republic of the Orange Free State. At the start of the Anglo-Boer War, John joined the Bloemfontein Commando, and went on to fight in the great battles of

Modder River, Magersfontein and Paardeberg. He was one of only a handful of burghers who managed to break out of General Cronje's trapped laager at Paardeberg, but was captured shortly afterwards. After the fall of Bloemfontein, he took the Oath of Allegiance to the British Crown, only to be rearrested and sent to a POW camp in Cape Town, after his boyish boasts, about what he would do to Field Marshal Lord Roberts were he still to be in the field with a gun in his hand, were overheard and reported. Like his still-to-be-born nephew Stan Smollan, he attempted to escape; unlike Stan, he did not succeed, as one of the collaborators in the venture betrayed the group's plans at the last minute. John was then shipped off to Ceylon, where he and thousands of other Boer prisoners sat out what was left of the war. On his return to South Africa, he became a model citizen, including serving a term as Mayor of Kuruman. He also served in the Union Defence Force during World War I, attaining the rank of Captain."

BACK IN SOUTH AFRICA

Within 30 days of setting out from Anzio, Stan and his companions were flown by the South African Air Force to Waterkloof Airbase in Pretoria.

The base was established in 1938, initially as a practice forced landing field, secondary to Swartkop. During those years, the airfield measured 1775 x 1550 yards of grass landing strip, which was typical and adequate for aircraft types of the 1930's and 1940's.

A warm official welcome reception awaited the four lads. Their parents had been invited. It was near the end of the week, and they were front-page news in the *Sunday Times*, the largest Sunday newspaper in South Africa.

That same month, the *Rand Daily Mail*, a leading Johannesburg daily paper (for whom Bill Berridge had worked prior to the war) published a full report on the affair entitled: "Stirring Story of Springboks' Escape'. It was noted that the four were the first escaped South Africans to rejoin the Allied forces then engaging the Germans in that area.

Back home, the now free POW escapees, were given three months military leave. After that they received instructions to proceed to Military College to be interviewed personally by Brigadier Klopper at Roberts Heights.

For some reason, they did not meet Brigadier Klopper there. However, the lads did meet the legendary rugby Springbok, Danie Craven. They attended his gymnasium. They also underwent a Rehabilitation PT Course, at the Physical Training Branch of the South African Military College, headed by Lt-Col Danie Craven, until 1946.

Doc Craven wanted them to be examined by a Psychiatrist, a Physician and a Pathologist. Royce Schulman commented that the four escapees must be considered mad or to have ulcers. Stool samples were requested of the four.

They put the stool samples under the barracks floor and, only two weeks later, handed them in to the pathologist.

The report came back "*No sign of life!*"

Stan Smollan wearing his new civilian clothes, after
being honourably discharged from the army in 1944

HONOURABLE
MILITARY DISCHARGE

Stan's medals

Officially, the lads were still part of the armed forces, but after they had been put through psychological and physical tests, the decision was made to honourably discharge them, and to return them to civilian life.

Stan recalled:

We were duly paid out our accumulated army pay at 3"6d (three shillings and sixpence) per day, plus £37.10 to buy a new outfit of clothes and "that, for us, was that!" For thousands of other South African POWs, however, many long months of captivity still lay ahead. We took the money to a nearby friend, Willie Michael, who owned a clothing shop, and he kitted us out each with a Summrie jacket for an additional £1 per month.

I lived with my mother's sister, Hannah Lewis. The four of us met up at my mother's house in Killarney and we walked to the bus stop. We climbed onto a bus and we were performing in a rowdy fashion. A woman with an umbrella accosted us, and said we were a disgrace, and should "join the army like other decent boys"!

POST WAR
RE-ESTABLISHMENT

Sadly in changing from a military life back to a civilian life, the discharged soldiers had to return to reality and responsibility. This led to severing some friendships. They encountered some failed and some successful adjustments. If Stan was approached for a loan of £5, he would say "Ï only have £3 and you don't have to pay it back."

Later Stan was to be instrumental in an attempt, through contacts in the South African military, to secure the release of Tommaso de Lellis, whose family had been so kind to Stan and his companions.

De Lellis had been offered employment or repatriation - both achievable. Stan had arranged with Lieutenant-Colonel Danie Craven and Major-General Klopper for this offer to be made. De Lellis declined on a point of honour for his men. He would stay with his men while they were still in captivity. Stan corresponded with and visited the de Lellis family after the war and renewed the acquaintanceship.

Stan went back to his pre-war employers at OK Bazaars (1929) Limited, who had paid him, via his mother, £11 per month for three and a half years. However, Stan told me that at the time he was unsure of himself, in a competitive position. He thus asked Michael Miller, (co-managing director of OK) to release him.

Stan then joined his father's insurance business. At that stage the family business was not really able to sustain another partner.

In August 1947 Stan married my mother, Ruth Perlman, a divorcee with a daughter, Arlene. I was born in September 1948.

Dad's wartime friend Harry Kahn, was a prominent sportsman and baseballer. On the occasion of my birth, my parents got a telegram from Harry and his wife Hadassah. It read:

UP THE SECOND JOCKS AND TARHUNA BOYS. HEARTIEST CONGRATULATIONS TO BOTH OF YOU. TONS OF LUCK. HADASSAH AND HARRY KAHN.

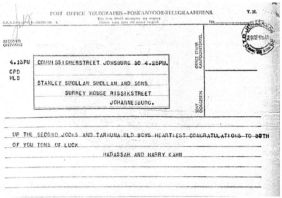

Stan worked for his cousin Fred Smollan for a time. Then he was recruited by Herbert Landau, to become managing Director of Landau and Coetsee Ltd., which, uncharacteristically for that type of high risk business, sustained very few casualties under Stan Smollan's watch.

After the death of Herbert Landau in 1957, Stan's association with the late Abe Schwartz, one of the leading Chartered Accountants of the day, led to The Elephant Trading Company taking Landau & Coetsee Limited into its trading and finance empire. Stan was retained as managing director.

In the 1980's, Stan left to become Managing Director of Brown Brothers Shipping Company Limited.

In 1989 Brown brothers was sold to "Arab Asian Bank of Bahrain". Stan duly went to London, and met the new owners. He continued as managing director, until shortly afterwards when he decided to retire from   Brown Brothers.

In the meantime, in February 1989, Stan had formed his own private company called Sarrand cc., In recent years ownership of Sarrand changed hands.

In 1953, my parents were on a trip to England to view the coronation parade of Queen Elizabeth II, from Herbert Landau's flat in Park Lane, London. There they met Stan's cousin, Flight Lieutenant, Henry George (Harry) Hyams of the RAF in Middlesborough. Harry Hyams immigrated to South Africa at the age of 37. He and Stan went on to become very close lifelong friends. The late Harry produced a bound booklet for Stan's 90th birthday.

The Ministry of Defence in England were awarding a limited number of veteran medals to servicemen of WWII and after. As a result of Harry Hyams's determined and diligent efforts and persistence, there duly arrived an award, personally delivered to Stan in the form of a pin-medal in a jewellery box. With it was a certificate from the Under-Secretary of Defence at Whitehall.

Stan Smollan's True WW2 Saga   **Escape To Anzio**

The Certificate of Service states that Stanley Smollan enlisted on the 13th July 1940 as a full time volunteer to serve in the Second Transvaal Scottish, and that he was honourably discharged on the 1st November 1944. Thus in 2006, Stan Smollan was presented with Her Majesty's Armed Forces Veteran's Badge by the UK Ministry of Defence.

Stan Smollan & Harry Hyams at Stellenbosch University

Stan dedicated the award to the other members of the quartet who made their successful bid for freedom, Royce Schulman, Colin Stewart and Bill Berridge.

Brothers, Paul and David Brokensha, were prisoners of war with Stan. Their father was a judge of the Supreme Court of Natal, and a personal friend of General Jan Smuts. After the war, David won a bursary to Cambridge University. He went on to become a famous anthropologist and university Professor.

I was privileged to meet David, when he travelled from Fishhoek to Johannesburg to attend Dad's 90th birthday party. Stan and David had last seen each other in 1954, over 50 years before. At Stan's 90th birthday party, he quoted the following piece from his own book *Brokies Way*.

"I do distinctly recall being presented with a greatcoat by Stan Smollan in about September, when the desert nights were beginning to get chilly. When it was cold, Paul and I shared one blanket, snuggling up to keep warm, and the greatcoat was a blessing. Stan, one of the few POWs who did not smoke, bartered cigarettes for this greatcoat for me. When he gave it to me, I had to try hard not to weep, it was one of the most welcome presents I have ever had, and one of the most disinterested gestures I have known, a pure act of love. (Paul and I met Stan again after the war, at the Wanderers Club in Johannesburg: he had become a successful businessman.)"

This act of generosity is indicative of how Dad has conducted himself throughout his life.

Stan Smollan and David Brokensha at Stan's 90th birthday
celebration – 10th January 2010

Stan continued to maintain a close association with the Transvaal Scottish. In March 2009, he was invited to lay the wreath on the Memorial Day for the First, Second and Third Transvaal Scottish Regiments in memory of the Regiment's activities in Abyssinia, Sidi Rezegh and Sollum.

On a lighter note, until recently, he participated in the annual regimental bowls tournament between   the Transvaal Scottish, the Sappers (South African Engineer Corps) and the Gunners. and he was the only   Second World War veteran still playing.

The Jock Column, September 2008:
'There was a poignant moment during the celebrations, when Stan Smollan (2TS) received a standing ovation when Paddy Clarence presented him with a set of regimental cufflinks and tie pin for valiant effort. Stan then at the tender age of 89 and the only Transvaal Scottish WW2 veteran playing in the competition, committed himself to playing all eight gruelling games without a whimper.'

In his younger years, prior to taking up lawn bowls, Stan was a regular golfer at Killarney Golf Club, of Gary Player fame. He achieved a "HOLE-IN-ONE" on the 18th of February 1961.

Stan Smollan (far left) at
The Battle of Sollum, 50th Anniversary

Stan was destined to become a member of yet another 'quartet' - one of the Wanderers' Bowling Club's four oldest active members. Since the other three had turned a hundred, whereas he was still *only* in his nineties, he was known as the 'baby' of the group. With the passing of Norman Gordon, the Jewish Springbok cricketer of 'Timeless Test' fame, the quartet became a trio, till Stan retired from bowls.

Stan asked me to mention a few Transvaal Scottish Sportsmen of note :
  Trefall Werge Talbot Baines, *Springbok Cricketer*
  George Brunton, *Springbok Soccer Player*
  R A 'Bob' Curnow, *Springbok Cricketer*
  Paul Loeser, *Springbok Cricketer*
  Owen E WYNNE, *Springbok Cricketer*

Escape To Anzio

Paddy Clarence, Jeff Smollan, Stan Smollan and Bob Prince after lunch at Transvaal Scottish Regimental HQ "The View", July 2015

On Friday 7 November 2014 two wreath laying ceremonies took place at the Wanderers Main Clubhouse Memorial Wall. The first wreath was laid by Mr Stan Smollan, who has been a member of the Wanderers Club for almost 80 years. Both Stan and the layer of the second wreath ended their speeches with the words:

"We Will Remember Them"

CORRESPONDENCE

Rough translations of correspondence with and about Italian families that befriended Stan Smollan during his *ESCAPE TO ANZIO*.

As I was finishing research for this book, Dad insisted that he be quoted as follows:

"I must emphasize that to this day, I have a warm affection and respect for the Italian people and soldiers that I met and/or corresponded with."

Stan went on to say that there may have been contrary views given by certain people, who had their own circumstances to consider.

The Italians who helped the four, gave them each Italian names:

Bill Berridge was called *Guilwelmo*.
Royce Schulman was called *Romalo*.
Colin Stewart was called *Nicolino*
Stan was called *Stanislao* and *Stanislavo*.

My Dear friends,   ROME 17/3/1944

I am answering your lovely letter, from which I learned about your very good health, and I am happy to inform you that my family and I are doing well also. Just that I am very sorry that you didn't get our news, this being our third letter we sent to you, hoping that you will receive it.

We thank you with all our heart for your lovely thoughts, and it will be a pleasure for us if you can write to us more often. We did all we could to keep in touch with you. I only ask you again, and sorry I have to repeat, to write us more often. About your colleagues Bruno and Enrico we have no more news, and we didn't even receive any news about them from the Institute of Liberation, Rome. To the people that were parents in those very difficult times, we wish them all the best and all the happiness.

All our family remind you that we always hope to meet again, to tell all the beautiful stories. From my wife Lida, and from my daughters Maria, Aristea, Giovanna, receive the best wishes.

And from my part all the best.

Your friend always CORSETTI

ORFEO

PW INFORMATION BUREAU
HQ EAST AFRICA COMMAND.

EAC/PWIB/3/3571
14th April 1944.

The Controller,
Prisoner of War Information Bureau,
Johannesburg.

Copy to Principal Information Officer, MOI Nairobi. ref:
D/2/1/22? of 8th April 1944.

Corporal MAGGIORE DE LELLIS.

Ref: your enquiry dated 29th March, 1944 addressed
to this Bureau and received by MOI

It is regretted that it is impossible to identify
positively the POW enquired for from the information
supplied by you as we have no record of a Cpl. Maggiore
DE LELLIS and no prisoner of this name who shows an
address at GERANO.

Given below however, are particulars of all POW of this
surname recorded with us, and also the name of one
evacuee who might possibly be the man enquired for :--

1.   EAF/62765 Capitano DE LELLIS Carlo.
      Born Mirabello Sannitico 1/4/89.
      Father Pasquale. Mother: Carmela
      Next of kin: DE LELIS Agostina, wife Campobasso

2.   EAF/64338 Soldato DE LELLIS Felice
      Born Pastina. 15/5/15
      Father Michele. Mother Pasqualina
      Next of kin. Father, Pastina (Frosinone)

3.   EAF/57714 Serg. Magg. DE LELLIS Luigi
      Born. Pedinonte Alife. 19/10/13.
      Father Fiorenzo. Mother Augusta
      Next of kin DE LELLIS Alfonso, brother Piedimonte D'Alife
                                                (Benevento.)

4.   ME/273160 Milite Forestale DE LELLIS Tommaso:
      Born Tivoli 9/11/97
      Father Luigi   Mother Virginia   Lielli
      next of kin DE LELLIS Lina   Wife Modena
      above POW transferred S.Africa 15/1/44

5.   Evacuee 5098 DE LELLIS Mario
      Mother Maria, Piazza Municipale 35, Pasterna, Frosinone.

Escape To Anzio

Dear Stanislao,   **Montario Romano 29.9.44**
Today I got two letters from you, and in one I got your photos. I am extremely happy that you got back home safely, where everybody waited for you, with all their love. I hope you found your mother in good form and healthy. Biasima and I pray for her. These letters mean that we are always thinking of each other. My daughter, Zita, Pierino, Anna, Emmer and others think of you all the time and we all receive your wishes very gladly.

Biasimo and I were very worried, and praying all the time that God would keep you safe and that you would go home soon. When we had good news about you and Nicolino, what happiness we felt. There are no words.

My wife and I wanted, within our budget, to organize a party for your birthday on the 10th of January, but your leaving took this joy away. However, now that we know that you are well and at home with your dearest ones, we are happy again. I wish I could be a bird, and fly to your house and to your window and give you a lot of hugs, and see you and talk to you, but this is just a dream, and we live with the hope that one day, soon, we will meet in one of the countries, mine or yours.

The situation in Montario was very difficult. A letter in your handwriting made us translate. There I found news about you from my daughter. She told me that you arrived home safe, and I was very happy to hear from you that Nicolino is ok also. I didn't receive anything from him, maybe because of the post.

If you can please send all our best to him as well, and lots of wishes from Enrico, Basilia, Bruno and Renato. Your italian mother and father send you a lot of best wishes, and send you lots of kisses and hugs.

Our son also sends you all best wishes
                    Atillio & Biasima

D.D 126 B.

*If you are paid, on understanding answer
to enclosed to reply all*
En reply please quote

A.G.(POW) 28/8

Tel. 21031 - Ext. 503

UNIE VAN SUID-AFRIKA—UNION OF SOUTH AFRICA

HOOFKWARTIER.
UNIE-VERDEDIGINGSMAG.

HEADQUARTERS
UNION DEFENCE FORCES,
PRETORIA.

2 Oct 44.   - 2-10-1944

27498 Pte S. Smollan
9 Killarney Court,
Killarney,
JOHANNESBURG.

POW 273180 DE LELLIS Tommasso.

1.   Your letter of 16 Sep 44, refers.

2.   It is regretted that the a/m POW is not available
for Outside Employment.

Colonel.
Brig-Gen.
A/ADJUTANT-GENERAL.

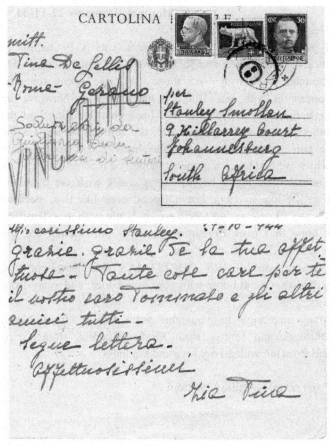

My Dear Stanley   **9-10-1944**

Thank you, thank you for your kindness. Best wishes and all the best to you, and for our dear Tommaso and to the other friends.
Affectionately
Aunt Tina

Escape To Anzio

Montario Romano 22-11-44

Dear Stanislao

I received two of your letters. I was very happy to receive your news, and to see that you remember us. My thoughts are always on those days we spent together, sometimes with fear. But it is all gone now. Now we are at home, safe and sound. We hope that Nicolino and the others are all at home and safe, the same as we are. I wrote to you once already, and in the letter I sent you a photo which we had taken together. I hope you received it.

Soon it is going to be Christmas and I wish we could be together like in 1943, but it's good even like this, because we are all celebrating Christmas at home with our families. I hope that over Christmas you will think about me, the way we will also think of you.

Wishing you MERRY CHRISTMAS. We also hope you will always be at home with your loved ones, and away from war.

Many greetings to you and your family from Nena, Giuseppe and Emma, from Mother Biagina, from Pietro and from me with all my love and kindness.

Papa (Dad) – Attilio Venettoni

D.D. 125.

In reply please quote

If ack or piot an understandly number as authored is termal

No. A.G.(POW) 29.

Telegraphic Address } " DEAGEN."
Telegramadres

PHONE: 21031 Ext. 505

UNION OF SOUTH AFRICA.–UNIE VAN SUID-AFRIKA.

OFFICE OF THE ADJUTANT GENERAL.
KANTOOR VAN DIE ADJUDANT-GENERAAL.

UNION DEFENCE FORCES.
UNIE–VERDEDIGINGSMAG.

PRETORIA.

29 Aug 45.

S.S. Smollan Esq.,
P.O. Box 3769,
JOHANNESBURG.

Sir,

ITALIAN POW 273180 DE LELLIS TOMMASO.

With reference to your letter dated 22 Aug 45, I have the honour to advise you that the question of giving some priority in repatriation to this POW whose family assisted you in your escape, will receive consideration. It is possible that within his appropriate group he may receive some preference.

As regards giving him money, it is pointed out that PsOW on final repatriation will not be permitted to take with them Union currency. On the other hand, money received by them during captivity can be credited to their account and this credit can be used by them for transfer to their families in Italy. Similarly, any money in their possession at the final repatriation will be credited to their account and will presumably be received by them from the Italian Government after arrival in Italy. You may therefore wish to take some advantage of these facts.

As far as clothing is concerned, this office is now in communication with Director General of Supplies with a view to laying down a list of such articles as PsOW may be permitted to purchase in the Union and take with them to Italy. This matter is not as yet finalised, but it is confidently expected that some permission will be granted in connection with the matter. If you wish, I can at a later stage furnish you with a list of the articles which may be authorised.

I have the honour to be,
Sir,
Your obedient servant,

COL.
ADJUTANT GENERAL.

Stanislao, my dear

Father Christmas is coming and I wish you and all your family everything you wish for. I hope that you will think of us also, and that Jesus Christ will bring you all joy and happiness.

I also wish that you and your family will always be together.

From Nena, Giuseppe, Antonia and Barbara.

Greetings with love, wishes and kisses from Attilio, Pietro andBiagina

Montario 29-11-1945

MERRY CHRISTMAS

Dear Stanislavo,

I cannot continue, if I do not send you my news, especially now that Christmas is coming.

We are all fine and we hope you are all the same. I wish I could fly to see you again. I send you happy birthday wishes for the 10th of January. I don't know if you get the post, because we wrote to you so many times, and we didn't get any answer. I send a lot of

wishes and greetings to Romalo and Guilwelmo. Can you send me news about Nicolino and Renato, because I don't know anything about them anymore. We will never forget you.

Lots of wishes for you, for your father, brothers and your niece.

Wishes and kisses from Pietro, mother Biacina and father Attilio

17 December 45

P. O. Box 3769,

JOHANNESBURG.

9th September, 1946.

Capt. Charlton,
Admin. Head Quarters,
Italian P.O.W. Camp,
ZONDERWATER.

Dear Sir,

     I enclose copies of correspondence with G.H.Q.
in connection with P.O.W. de Lellis, which will no
doubt be brought to your notice.

     Thanking you for your kind assistance,

               Yours faithfully,

                   S. S. SMOLLAN
             (2nd Transvaal Scottish).

THIS SPACE FOR POST OFFICE USE ONLY.—HIERDIE RUIMTE SLEGS VIR POSKANTOORGEBRUIK.
                                         No.

Sent 9/9/46   *Copy.*

POST OFFICE TELEGRAPHS—POSKANTOOR-TELEGRAAFDIENS,

Chks. Kas.	Office of Origin—Kantoor van Herkoms	Words. Woorde	Code. Kode.	Service Instructions. Diensaanwysings.	Sent. Oorgesein.

TO / AAN   *Signorina de Lellis Tora*
     Serano - Rome - ITALY.

*Romolo Gualdiero and myself saw Tommaso Is fit and
well. We are looking after him Endeavouring
to fix early return home*

            Stanislao Smollan

FROM / VAN

NOT TO BE TELEGRAPHED—MOENIE OORGESEIN WORD NIE.

Signature of Sender   Address
Handtekening van afsender   Adres.
N.B.—The Department is not liable for losses incurred through incorrect transmission, delay or non-delivery of telegrams.   L.W.—Die Departement is nie vir verliese gely as gevolg van onjuiste oorseining, vertraging of nis-aflewering van telegramme, aanspreeklik nie.

G.P.-S.8713—1943-6—100,000-100. S.   T. 28 (c).

P.O. Box 3769,

JOHANNESBURG.

8th October, 1946.

The Camp Commandant,
Italian Prisoner of War Camp,
ZONDERWATER.

Dear Sir,

I thank you for your letter of the 2nd instant
re P.C.W. de Lellis.

It is regrettable that a negative attitude has been
taken up by de Lellis.

However, will you accept and direct to Captain
Charlton my appreciation of all the assistance rendered in
investigating this case.

Yours faithfully,

S. SMOLLAN.

Farm Carolina 8 Nov 1946

Dear Mr Smollan,

The letter from you was sent to me here in Zonderwater. I believe you were disappointed because my signature of cooperation was missing, but it was a conditional promise and I decided not to sign it. It was a humiliation for me and at the same time desperation, after my interrogation. It was very frustrating for me hearing that the interest of the command was not about me, but about my family. I suggest my family to accommodate you. Again sorry for my attitude and hopefully in the future our good relation will be the same.

Here it is not too bad. The small amount of freedom, at the moment, is enough. After 5 long years in the cage, we breathe the smell of freedom. The location is about 6 miles from Carolina, and there is nothing interesting, but anyway it is not too bad.

I am begging you again Mr Smollan, don't bother to send me more food again. You have done enough for me. I have one request. Can I get a little tube of painting oil, for my spare time? Last month I got post from my sister. She said she got your telegram and 2 boxes full of sweets, and she went to visit my daughter who was delighted to enjoy your sweets.

Once again thanks so much from my sister Tina and myself.

I will meet you before my repatriation.

My regards to Romalo and Nicolino. And regards to all your families.

Tommaso de Lellis.

Dear Mr Smollan,

I received your letter, which was actually sent to Carolina. As you see I have again re-entered Zonderwater for repatriation for 24 hours, and then I'll go to Pietermaritzburg. I don't know how many days I will be there for, but we heard that we should embark in Durban on the 29th. I was assigned to 9 Gruppa (group).

Finally my day of freedom has arrived, and I think you can imagine how much I wait to finally hold my loved ones in my arms again.

I was very happy to hear that we will see you again in Italy, and I hope it will be soon. I don't know where I'll get my residency papers from. anyway I'll pass through Gerano first.

MERRY CHRISTMAS to you, to Romalo and Nicolino and all your families.

Lovely wishes and we will see you in Italy

Your's,

Tommaso De Lellis,

22-11-1946

MONTARIO ROMANO 17-11-1947

Dear Stanilavo

I can't continue if I don't write to you, especially near Christmas and the Easter holidays. It's a long time since I got any news from you. I hope you are all in good health, you, your father, your brothers.

Pietro has a new fiancé, and her name is Luisa. Greetings to you and your family.

Mother, father & Pietro say hello.

MERRY CHRISTMAS

Tivoli
23 November 1947
Dear Stanislao,
In March I sent you a letter describing the repatriation trip from Zonderwater back home, and the feeling that I had when I hugged, my family after so many years of absence. But I didn't get an answer from you.
I told you in the letter that I wanted to see you again, with all my pleasure, in Volpone, actually this summer I was hoping to find news about you coming to visit me. Even Tina sends a letter together with my letter, in which she thanks you for all the gifts you sent. Some packages came without the address or name, but I am sure they were from one of you. Thank you again.
To Romalo & Nicolino and yourself and your families. I hope you are all good. I and mine are desperate.
Please remember that we are waiting for you, and you are more than welcome, and with you Romalo and Nicolino also. But, I think it is better to come in springtime or summer time.

This time last year, we had news of repatriation. After more than five years we were finally free. Pietermaritzburg was disastrous, hunger, hunger and more hunger.
Now everything is over and we are in Italy, in this poor Italy, which cannot find peace yet. The economy is very bad and I think before going back to normal, it is going to be a long time.
I am in Tivoli (20km from Gerano) with my wife and the children, for their studies (school). Gerano is in elementary school and Luigino attains averages. Toto and Tina are in Volpone, and they are fine.

You are in Summer time, we have winter now, but we still have nice sunny days.

My dear Stanislao, sometimes we talk about so many other things but I'm sure you will keep the promise of your visit. Now I'm sorry about my daring but it is possible to send me some milk the condensed one, and some cigarettes and I'm thanking you for that beforehand.

I wish your families the best for the next Christmas holidays, (from my family also.).

Yours sincerely.

I shake and embrace your hands Yours

TOMMASO De Lellis Piazza

Deminario no 10 TIVOLI

(ROMA)

Montario 29.1.48

Dear Stanislao,

After some delay we send you our good news. We are in very good health. We hope please God that you are the same. Some days ago, we received your long awaited letter and we were very, very happy. We are happy to hear that you got married and you have a lovely baby girl. We are happy to hear all the great news you sent us in your letter. Please don't think that we forgot about yo,u because you are far away from us, because is not true. Our bodies are far away is true but our hearts are, and will be always together the same as when we were together in the tavern where we slept for so long.

My kind lady Ruth I send you our thanks for your beautiful thoughts you send to us, We have no words for that, just that we are waiting for you here to meet you in person, in our house.

In your letter you told us that you sent a package also, but we didn't get it yet, but we thank you very much for that.

Please receive many greetings from Father and Mother and Pietro

Good Health from Pietro's fiancé, Sister Lisa

Good health from   Miss Fioravanta – ZITA

Rome 15 June 1975

Dear Stanislao,

First of all I would like to apologise for my delay in writing to say thank you for your kindness to send me via my friend Buik, the file with all the copies we shared during my imprisonment, and after my repatriation. I was very pleased to read all of them again, but I really have to say that it upset me because it reminded me of the bad and very hard time, which will take me a long time to forgive. I really appreciate the little paper square with your pictures in the corner and even your wife, and I wish to meet you very soon.

I even appreciate your effort and your patience to find me in the P.O.W. camp. And the proof of your kindness, is a lot of contact between you and the command POW of Kenya and South Africa. And your interest for me to C.R. when I got transferred the last two months in the cage of Carolina. In Kenya and South Africa. I've experienced too much kindness but I never met another De Lellis, even if we were five. Barbara Yurgen told me how pleased they were when y met about the satisfaction of finding each other. ears ago I went to the Embassy of South Africa where they gave me an address, and I sent a letter to you, but I believe you never got it, otherwise you would have answered me. Above all I say that I wish to meet you very soon, and you said in your letter, if it is correctly translated, that it was a pleasure. I wish though that it could happen (that we meet) in Rome.

For many reasons, it is impossible for me to go to South Africa. So the Smollan family need to travel to Italy, to meet the De Lellis family in Rome.

You will even go to Gerano, where I have a house in a small countryside in Volpone, where we were together with Romalo and Nicolino for a very few days, 32 years ago. In those days the little house in Volpone was a hovel, and now it is brand new, with electricity, water and gas. Then if Mr and Mrs Smollan would like to, they could stay there for few days quietly. I would be very pleased to give you the house. After that we will have a long chat (unfortunately) in Italian.

And I would like to finish with best regards to you and your wife from me and my children. Hope to see you soon.   *De Lellis Tommasso*

9-12-1946
My Dear Stanislao,
Sincerely for Christmas I write to you and your family.
Together Pietro, Attilio and I wish you all the best
TINA
Montario Romano